Bob Bailey

Meeting Jesus the Christ Again

Meeting Jesus the Christ Again

A Conservative Progressive Faith

ROBERT A. CHESNUT

WIPF & STOCK · Eugene, Oregon

MEETING JESUS THE CHRIST AGAIN
A Conservative Progressive Faith

Wipf & Stock
An Imprint of Wipf and Stock Publishers
199 W. 8th Ave., Suite 3
Eugene, OR 97401

www.wipfandstock.com

PAPERBACK ISBN: 978-1-5326-1814-7
HARDCOVER ISBN: 978-1-4982-4345-2
EBOOK ISBN: 978-1-4982-4344-5

Manufactured in the U.S.A.   06/07/17

Dedicated with love and gratitude, blessings and prayers for . . .
Our children and their spouses: Andrew and Fabiola, Elizabeth and Paul;
And our grandchildren: Vanessa and Nicholas, David and Eric.

O God, who wonderfully created, and yet more wonderfully restored, the dignity of human nature: Grant that we may share the divine life of him who humbled himself to share our humanity, your Son Jesus Christ; who lives and reigns with you, in the unity of the Holy Spirit, one God, for ever and ever. *Amen.*

Book of Common Prayer (1979),
Preface of the Epiphany, 252 no. 4

... [I]n him all things hold together.

Col 1.17b

Contents

Acknowledgements

FOR SOME YEARS NOW, every night before retiring, my wife Jan and I have made a practice of naming at least three blessings for which we are thankful from the day past. At the very top of my all-time list of thanksgivings, just after God's grace, I would place Jan herself. Since we first met over 60 years ago as freshmen in a geology lab at the College of Wooster, she has faithfully offered me her loving support and encouragement, all the while striving to keep me honest and humble. An assiduous reader, she informs and entertains our family and me with the wonders and delights of the many worlds she explores in the many pages she turns. She has not only read and helped me to improve this work; she has also patiently endured my mental absence, even obsession, while I brought it to completion.

How far back does an author's indebtedness go? For me it is often traced all the way back, in the words of one of my favorite hymns ("For the Beauty of the Earth"), to gratitude "for the love that from our birth over and around us lies;" for "brother, sister, parent, child;" for "friends on earth and friends above." My gratitude extends to all the congregations, parishioners, staff, and pastors in places where Jan and I have served and been nurtured in faith, where we have ministered and been ministered unto. Some of them are named in this book, as are the College of Wooster in Wooster, Ohio, Harvard Divinity School, and Harvard University, where I have studied and been blessed by learned and devoted professors and fellow students.

I have acknowledged my gratitude in this book to authors who have enriched both my earlier as well as my more recent explorations of the faith that is examined and professed in these pages. Members of the Gayton Kirk Presbyterian Church (U.S.A.) here in Richmond, Virginia, who read and discussed an earlier version of the manuscript helped me to develop and clarify my thought. How blessed I am to have other friends and family who were willing to devote their time and careful attention to reading all or portions of the manuscript. I thank them wholeheartedly for their insightful suggestions and absolve them completely for the shortcomings that remain. In addition to Jan, they are: The Rev. Dr. Charles W. Brockwell, Jr., Dr. R. Andrew Chesnut, the Rev. Hunter R. Hill, the Rev. Dr. Sandra Hack Polaski, the Rev. Dr. Rebecca Harden Weaver, and the Rev. J. David Wiseman.

Finally, many thanks to our Pastor Janet James of the Gayton Kirk. She has invited me again and again to teach and preach (two of those sermons are appendices here), even while knowing that some of my thoughts might unsettle some of her flock.

Introduction

I SIMPLY COULD NOT believe it. In the week just before the 2016 election I found myself in conversation with an individual I had never met before. He was the new manager of the firm that serves the homeowners association of our suburban Richmond neighborhood and someone with whom I, as an officer of the association, would have to work rather closely in the months ahead. In the course of an hour-long, largely business-related conversation, our religious and political perspectives emerged. Having learned that I was a retired Presbyterian minister, he asserted that he had brought his Presbyterian parents over from the "dark side" to his own Assembly of God faith. I had hoped he was joking, but later he referred to my preferred candidate for president as "evil," "Satan," and an "agent of death." He could not understand, he said, how any Christian could possibly support her.

Given views such as this, is mutually respectful dialogue a possibility? God knows it is desperately needed. In all honesty, however, I could have said very similar things about his candidate . . . though I did not. With all the vitriolic polarization that accompanied the 2015–16 presidential campaign—and that seems likely to face us now for many years to come—this is, without doubt, a painfully difficult, complicated, challenging question for all who care about the health and well-being of our congregations, our communities, and our nation as a whole. How do we heal? How do we build bridges—especially if each side views the other as the embodiment of evil?

In a *Time* magazine interview about his new book *The First Love Story: Adam, Eve, and Us*, Bruce Feiler was asked: "Religion today is often used as a barrier—against the threat of terrorism or as a reason not to provide someone with a service. What do you make of that?"

Feiler replied: "We all have to get over that thing our mom told us: 'Don't talk about politics and religion in public.' The majority of people have yearnings and big questions and want to believe, but also want to coexist with people with whom they may also disagree, with whom they may also be sharing a bed or a table or a child. Those of us who are open-minded have to claim the microphone."[1]

Exactly! But, with my own strong convictions and equally strong inclinations to speak my mind, I must confess that I have found this a life-long challenge. From an early age I have had a keen interest in these two topics that together give rise to so much disagreement and discord—politics and religion. I have a second-grade school picture of myself sporting a Dewey for President campaign button—at a time when my home state of Oklahoma was about as solidly Democratic as it now is Republican. As a high school sophomore, having initially supported Sen. Robert A. Taft of Ohio for the Republican presidential nomination in 1952, I then undertook to organize a Youth for Eisenhower Club that was far more active locally than either of the political parties. We even landed a story on the front page of *The Elk City Democrat*, a weekly newspaper that came out in support of Ike. Over the years, however, my views have evolved from those of a teenage fan of Sen. Joseph McCarthy to those of a Bernie Sanders Democrat. Nevertheless, from that day to this, I have not wavered in my conviction that both religion and politics are of vital concern to human well-being, that Aristotle was right in defining politics as the science of the common good, and that our faith ought to shape our political goals and methods.

As intimated in the paragraphs above, the reader will find many allusions in this book to my evolving views, my faith journey, and pastoral experiences—offering something of a theological memoir along the lines of Marcus Borg's *Convictions* and recent books by New Testament scholar Dale Allison, Jr. So I begin with a "Personal Prelude," which the reader may consider optional.

Within many of our congregations and denominations our divisions are, of course, about basic Christian beliefs, not only about politics, economics, and social issues such as gay marriage and abortion. Evangelical/conservative Christians charge that liberal/progressive Christians are soft on basic beliefs such as biblical authority, Christ's divinity, salvation through him alone, and the centrality of his cross. Liberal/progressive Christians, for their part, suspect that those "across the aisle" cherry-pick the Bible to support their biases on political, economic, and social issues, all the while ignoring the message of the prophets and Jesus about social justice and God's "preferential option" for those disadvantaged and oppressed.

1. Hopper, "8 Questions," 64.

Furthermore, progressives will ask: Isn't Christian exclusivism a real and present danger, not just in an increasingly religiously diverse America, but also in a world that desperately needs to bridge the gulfs that now produce bitter and violent conflict in the name of God?

Even with strong views on all sides, I do believe that within our faith communities we can and should set an example of striving for a center that will hold us together, a uniting core of faith that can enable us to find common ground with those who see things differently. On the few occasions during the 2016 campaign season when I have had an opportunity to preach, I have sought to show how basic biblical convictions underlie certain fundamental American values around which both liberals and conservatives can rally. Readers may judge for themselves how well that may have been accomplished by looking at the sermons in the Appendix. These were preached at our Presbyterian church here in suburban Richmond, a congregation with a diverse representation across the political and theological spectrum and with a few recent experiences of open discussion around potentially hot-button topics such as transgender identity and race relations.

I have also offered at this same church a course on social justice, using Jim Wallis's *On God's Side: What Religion Forgets and Politics Hasn't Learned About Serving the Common Good.*[2] Wallis, I believe, has done an excellent job laying out areas of potential common ground between liberals and conservatives who seek the common good, looking toward values and policies that are both individually responsible and socially just. But now, admittedly, with 81 percent of self-identified white evangelical Christians having voted for Donald Trump, it is clearer than ever that bridge-building efforts such as Wallis's will be both increasingly difficult to accomplish and all the more urgently needed. On the other hand, perhaps disillusionments to come may produce some soul-searching and reexamination of biblical and theological positions.

The political, social, and economic implications of Christian faith will certainly be given serious attention here, but the primary focus will be on finding theological common ground about core beliefs. Hot-button issues of the "culture wars," such as abortion and sexual identity/orientation, as intensely polarizing as they can be, are outside the purview of this book.

Chapter 1 affirms the need for both/and thinking and the wisdom of paradox, a perspective that is developed throughout the book. With the

---

2. Wallis, *On God's Side*, see especially chapter 8.

aim of building bridges between Christians left and right, the best in both progressive/liberal Christianity and evangelical/conservative Christianity is highlighted. But a hard look is often taken at where both can tend to go astray, so we can pull back from some of the extremes that threaten to pull Christians apart. It will seem at times that tough love is being applied to the discussion, but all the while I am trying always to speak the truth (as I understand it, of course) in love. Often the reader will need to finish a chapter before concluding where I come out on a particular topic.

Chapter 2, for example, begins by celebrating some of the outstanding values on the progressive side, but then turns to ask whether some leading progressive Christian thinkers may be in danger of abandoning essentials of traditional Christian belief.

Chapter 3 examines the perils of biblical literalism, how it may distract us from the Bible's core messages. A big-picture approach to biblical interpretation is needed, moving us beyond "sola scriptura" to a broader theological scheme of faith-formulation as suggested by John Wesley's quadrilateral of scripture, tradition, reason, and experience.[3]

Chapter 4 affirms the importance of understanding the nature of faith as foundational trust, reasoned belief, and faithful living. This provides the basis for what we may term "Neo-classical Christianity," enabling us to make good sense of old doctrines in ways that avoid some of their typical pitfalls, transcending a narrow Enlightenment rationalism while appealing to postmodern intellectual plausibility. As our congregations move toward identifying such a center for their faith, I know from experience that, at the same time, they can also be open enough to welcome and embrace within their extended church family others who may not yet find themselves in the same place theologically.

The following chapters offer a rethinking of several old dichotomies about traditional Christian beliefs:

- Chapter 5: The religion *of* Jesus or the religion *about* Jesus;
- Chapter 6: Personal salvation or the social gospel;
- Chapter 7: An impersonal versus a personal God;

---

3. My good friend and Wesley scholar the Rev. Dr. Charles W. Brockwell, Jr. reminds me that Wesley himself did not use the term "quadrilateral," which has since become commonplace in reference to his method. Also, instead of "tradition," Wesley spoke of "Christian antiquity," "creeds," "homilies," "Book of Common Prayer," and so forth as sources for the articulation of Christian belief.

- Chapter 8: Self-assertion/fulfillment or self-sacrifice and the way of the cross;

- Chapter 9: Original sin or original blessing;

- Chapter 10: Jesus as the fulfillment of Jewish expectations for the coming divine-human Son of Man/suffering-redeeming Messiah or the notion that this whole construct is a post-Jesus invention derived from Greek concepts;

- Chapter 11: Penal substitutionary atonement theory or Christ's death seen as only martyrdom without atoning significance;

- Chapter 12: Discomfort and/or indifference about evangelism or an impulse to save souls from hell through Christ alone;

- Chapter 13: Formulaic preoccupation with individual deliverance from hell or skepticism about anything at all beyond the grave.

Throughout, then, the goal is to build some bridges with solid biblical and traditional support toward a conservative/progressive or progressive/conservative center of Christian faith.

Above all else, Jesus the Christ and his cross are central here. His truth is honored by taking most seriously the search for the historical Jesus, embracing his full humanity and the importance of his teachings. But moving beyond the somewhat rather "literalistic" verse-by-verse skepticism so often characteristic of the Jesus Seminar approach, the focus instead is on the "big picture" of his life and teaching. This will point us toward, as key to understanding him, his call to life in the kingdom and to the self-sacrificial way of the cross. Yet it is not the self-abnegation of far Eastern religion he offers. It is the spiritually necessary death of the false self so that the true self may live. Jesus invites us to re-centered lives, fully integrated around ultimate loyalty and love of his very personal God, and in the love of our neighbors as ourselves. His is a humane, humanistic, humanitarian God. Beyond this, however, more recent scholarship provides grounds for a surprising new confidence that Jesus's postulated self-understanding as suffering servant, Son of Man, and divine/human Messiah derives from well-established Jewish traditions of his time, not from post-resurrection inventions originating from Greek categories.

While traditional Christian notions of original sin can be profoundly problematic in multiple ways, there is peril in abandoning the view that humanity is far from measuring up to its creation in the image and likeness of

God. Sin and evil are perversely and pervasively real. For various reasons, this realistic assessment of the human condition is necessary. To understand our universal human predicament as one of "alienating self-absorption" is to see clearly that each of us as individuals, as well as the whole of humanity, stands in need of healing, deliverance, and restoration to the goodness that God intends for us—lives that are re-centered in loving God with all our being, loving our neighbors as ourselves, and striving for a world of justice, shalom, and caring for all of creation. Toward this end, it is undeniably clear that we need a Savior.

The biblical figures Son of Man, Messiah, and new Adam offer a human/divine Jesus who comes to us as the embodiment of the restored humanity that is God's will for us from the beginning. Together with John's "vine and branches" image, we have here the foundations for a Christocentric body mysticism in which humanity is invited to participate in the human/divine Christ-nature. Jesus Christ is God's participation in our life so that we might participate in the divine life. But this participation involves a great crossing of the gulf of alienation created by sin. It is a crossing that Christ accomplishes for us through his incarnation, death, and resurrection, as he also calls us to participate in that crossing beginning with our own death/resurrection in baptism. The focus here is on participatory restoration rather than on penal substitution. The cross is about God's restorative justice, setting things right, a healing process much like the one that is required by recovery from addiction—a painful process of honest self-recognition; a passage through the worst; and a recognition of the consequences of our alienation so that we may come out whole on the other side. More than only doctrine and sacraments, more than just ideas, this saving process can and must be a lived reality of continual moral and attitudinal transformation, of dying to live.

Believers are called as the body of Christ to embody the good news as he did—faithfully fulfilling the same mission to which the Spirit had anointed him, bringing good news of healing and deliverance to the world. An example of this incarnational evangelism/mission is laid out here in some detail, exemplified in the life of one congregation that is especially familiar to the author. Such faithfulness may lead us, as it did Christ, to take up our own crosses.

Finally, consideration is given to Christian expectations for the coming of God's kingdom and what lies ahead after death. This will move beyond, on the one hand, the formulaic evangelical preoccupation with individual deliverance from hell through faith in Christ alone, and, on the other hand, the typical progressive skepticism about anything at all beyond this life. To claim the assurances of Jesus, of other scriptural promises, and the assertions of early Christian fathers is to affirm with them that all will be well, that God will finally set things right, restoring everyone and all things. Otherwise, how it is possible to assert, with any good faith whatsoever, that God is love? Hope also comes from certain evangelical thinkers who are now going so far as to sympathetically explore the possibility of universal salvation, affirming the notion of hell as ultimately redemptive or incorporating something like a "Protestant purgatory" into the process. Yes, the love and justice of God certainly require a divine judgment for all souls, but that judgment is, as the cross reveals, ultimately and comprehensively redemptive.

I have pointed above toward "striving for a center that will hold us together, a uniting core of faith that can enable us to find common ground with those who see things differently." In recent years, evangelicals in particular have engaged in discussions about whether unity is to be found through a "bounded set" or a "centered set." The difference between these two approaches has been explained by evangelical pastor John Ortberg by posing the question, "How do you keep the cattle on the ranch?" The bounded-set approach, according to Ortberg, is to build a fence around the ranch. The centered-set approach is to dig a well at the center of the ranch. In the final analysis, says Ortberg, it is not one or the other of these; it is both/and.[4] We need a well and we need fencing, the latter being some shared standards of belief and practice.

Both the centered and the bounded approaches receive their due in this book. But at the center must be the well, for it has the water without which there is no life. At our center is Jesus the Christ, who offered himself to the Samaritan woman at the well (John 4:1–41) as a "spring of water gushing up to eternal life." She, in turn, ran off to tell her neighbors about this amazing man, inviting and urging all to "Come and see." She shows us too that it's not only about getting those of us already on the ranch to stay there; it's also about inviting others to join us. Hers is the invitation found again and again in the pages of this book. Come and see. Come meet Jesus the Christ again. Find in his teachings, life, death, resurrection, and living presence the center of all things, the center of our faith communities, the center of our personhood.

4. Ortberg, "Category Confusion."

A Personal Prelude

IN A SMALL TOWN that straddled Route 66 in western Oklahoma, in a faithful, church-going family, in a conservative (but not self-consciously fundamentalist) Presbyterian congregation—there I grew to early maturity. There, in the fifteenth year of my life, I experienced a transformation that would prove profoundly pivotal—spiritual awakening, a call to ministry, foundations laid for all the years that have followed. There, in the late winter through spring of 1953, I found myself pushed from without and pulled from within to claim my inherited faith for my own. Deeply unhappy with my home life, unhappy with myself—in retrospect, in fact, I was depressed. Significantly overweight, bluntly assertive about my dogmatically held right-wing religious and political convictions, I found myself unpopular both with many of my peers and with adult authority figures . . . whose authority I was given to challenge.

Challenging authority, strongly held convictions strongly expressed— these character traits somehow emerged from an early age. I vividly recall, at about age five, rebuking an aunt for refusing to let her dog into her own house because he had muddy paws. "He has as much right to be here as you do," I declared. Shocked, my uncle turned to my father and asked, "What have you been feeding that boy, tiger meat?" Tiger meat aside, I can only say that I displayed a precocious identity with the underdog!

But then, where was I to go for help in the midst of my adolescent unhappiness? During the Lenten season of 1953 I turned to prayer, to fasting, and to the Bible. In an amazingly brief time, within just a few months, I was finding my life astonishingly transformed, body and soul. I do not hesitate to call it a conversion, a "born again," evangelical experience. Through a new-found self-discipline, empowered by prayer, I shed forty pounds from my bulging body. Through scriptural insights, I began to claim a new view of myself, of the new person God was calling me to be. Astonishingly, I

1

found Jesus calling me to pray for those I considered my antagonists, to lay aside my opinionated arrogance and take on humility, to listen patiently to those with whom I disagreed.

The crucible of my spiritual awakening came as I stood one night in the backyard of our home, arms outstretched to the deep, star-filled, western Oklahoma sky, pleading for divine deliverance. Suddenly I felt the love of God streaming down into my heart, assuring me that I was loved, affirmed. Whatever my faults and failures, I now knew that—by the love of God in Christ displayed upon the cross—my existence would forever bear a divine stamp of approval.

It was this new-found security in God's love that began to make it possible for me first to become self-critical, and then to embark on a course of change. A God-given ability to transcend myself, to see myself through God's eyes, to see how I needed to change and claim the power to work toward that change—these are the truly amazing spiritual gifts that grasped me at such a young age. And what made this conversion, this transformation, possible? Again, above all, it was the love of God, the experience and conviction found through scripture, prayer, and meditation that God loved me and accepted me just as I was, a love that God in Christ had displayed upon the cross. Whatever my faults and shortcomings, I now had a bedrock conviction that God had stamped an indelible seal of divine approval upon my very existence for all time and eternity. It was, in a few traditional words, "salvation by grace through faith" leading toward an ongoing "sanctification," the transforming process by which the Holy Spirit shapes us into more holy, Christ-like persons.

Yes, I had accepted Jesus Christ as my Lord and Savior. But in my own experience the order of that familiar profession was reversed. Christ as Savior came first for me, through the realization of God's amazing, saving grace in Christ. Because Christ came into my heart first as Savior, he then claimed me as Lord of my life. The "Savior part" of this spiritual experience I experienced as sudden, almost instantaneous. The "Lord part" of it, however, is progressive, unfolding. How vividly I still recall, even more than sixty years later, making a start on this transforming journey of accepting Christ as Lord. In my prayers, making purely intuitive use of a spiritual discipline that I would only much later learn to identify as "visualization," I would see myself offering up to God everything near and dear to me—all my attachments and desires, all the loves and loyalties of my life—as I simultaneously prayed for the courage and commitment to relinquish whatever might be necessary in order to make Christ indeed the Lord of my life, to put him first and foremost above all else, all others.

I recall reading somewhere that Dietrich Bonhoeffer first accepted Christ as Lord of his own life; that he then saw that Christ was Lord of the church; and that he finally came to know that Christ was the Lord of the world. I take that to mean that Bonhoeffer—not at first much involved in the church—moved from a personal, individual experience of Christ's Lordship to a more communal understanding of Christ's sovereignty within the community of faith, through which the experiences and perspectives of other believers, past and present, helped to shape his own faith. Finally, he realized that Christ was calling him to a costly discipleship within the world of a Nazi tyranny that claimed an idolatrous allegiance superseding all others.

Spiritual transformation does not happen overnight. Residual elements of the old self stubbornly hang on even as we move on. As I went off a few years later to the Presbyterian-related College of Wooster in Ohio, I was still clinging on to many of my old conservative, dogmatic certainties. All too soon, however, courses in the Bible and in evolution were challenging my fundamentalism. Courses in economics and history were shaking my economic and political views. Did God really, literally, create the world in six days? Was a dog-eat-dog capitalism really, truly, compatible with the teachings of the New Testament? These were painful questions to contemplate, questions that would shake the foundations of my previous worldview. But if Jesus Christ was truly my Lord, then didn't I have to finally let go of anything else that now began to appear as incompatible with my highest allegiance?

In some instances new insights came rather quickly. So, for example, by the end of my freshman year I would return home for the summer with a new and broader view of the inspiration and authority of scripture. What finally mattered was not that God created the world *in six days*, but that *God* created the world and created it *good*. Furthermore, God had given humans freedom to choose good from evil, a freedom that each of us in our self-centeredness tragically misused and abused.

Moreover, what came to matter most to me personally was a new realization that from the very beginning of the Bible's historic drama, we are presented with the story of a God who liberates the oppressed, who brings God's people out of darkness and slavery into a new birth of empowerment and self-determination guided by godly values and visions for their future.

This held extraordinary personal meaning and power for me because it was also the story of my own encounter, beginning at age fifteen, with this gracious God of deliverance. Much later it would open me to the power of Latin American liberation theology emerging from the contest of repressive military oligarchies in the 1960s, seventies, and eighties.

The transformation in my views at Wooster was also aided and abetted by an alluring young woman I met in a geology lab in our freshman year ... and later married within a week following our graduation in 1959. Janet Rippey, beautiful, well-read, and liberal, was from a New York community that was pretty much the polar opposite of mine in Oklahoma. Her hometown was the charming, sophisticated, solidly liberal hamlet of Palisades on the Hudson, just a few miles north of New York City. There she had grown to maturity in a faithful Presbyterian home with a portrait of FDR (a bête noir for my own father) prominently displayed on the living room wall.

In our sophomore year Jan and I, both majoring in religious studies, also took a course in evolution. The College of Wooster was one of the very first church-related colleges in the country to offer a course on that subject, much in keeping with its earliest tradition. Founded in 1866, the college seal then and now displays a telescope and an open Bible with a motto that declares, "Ex Uno Fonte." From one source—all truth is from one source, whether the Bible or science.

Other changes in my thinking would take years rather than months to unfold. However, by the time I graduated from Wooster and headed off to Harvard Divinity School, my social, economic, and political views had turned 180 degrees from when I entered college. Both my embrace of an Exodus theology and my reading of the teachings of Jesus and the rest of the New Testament had led me to conclude that God's special concern with the oppressed, the neglected, and the marginalized could not be reconciled with a system that afforded free rein to the rich and powerful, that "love your neighbor as yourself" and "bear one another's burdens" were incompatible with a philosophy of individualism that encourages a "dog eat dog and the devil take the hindmost" unfettered free enterprise.

Even though my early views and values were shaped in a quite conservative environment, belief in human equality and sympathy for the underdog have also been bedrock convictions of mine for as long as I can remember. This may have been in part due to my being the youngest by far of three brothers, feeling that I had to assert myself at home as an equal in a world of adult family members. In large measure, however, my early commitment to equality was thanks to the influence of my broadminded, tolerant mother—attitudinally out of place in our small town—who quietly questioned the intolerance of our culture on matters of racial inequality and discrimination. Never, ever did I hear her speak a negative word about another race, religion, or nationality.

Also, early on, I found myself fascinated by religious diversity. In high school I dated a Roman Catholic girl and was eager to explore the differences between her faith and my own. Later, one of the factors that drew me to Harvard Divinity School was the religious diversity of its faculty and student body. Through the years of my ministry I dreamt from time to time about the possibility of serving a far more diverse congregation than the ones in which I had thus far found myself. Finally, when I was fifty-one, that opportunity came—and came, I might say, with something of a vengeance! It came as a call to serve as Pastor of the historic inner-city East Liberty Presbyterian Church in Pittsburgh. The story of these final fourteen years of my ministry, 1988 to 2002, is told far more fully in my previous book, *Transforming the Mainline Church: Lessons in Change from Pittsburgh's Cathedral of Hope.*

Yes, the East Liberty Church offered "diversity with a vengeance"— black and white, rich and poor and everything in between, urbanites and suburbanites, liberals and moderates and conservatives, straights and gays, college and university and seminary professors plus some homeless folk residing in the shelter housed within our church building—a few of whom who could barely read or write—all side by side in our pews! On every hand I met culture shocks and challenges.

One hard reality I was soon to learn—and would continue to learn and relearn over the months and years—was what a social classist I had been without even knowing it. When I had led new-member orientation sessions in previous congregations, I had been accustomed to lifting up the Presbyterian emphasis on education, how Presbyterians had founded dozens upon dozens of college and universities over the years, and what a high percentage of Presbyterians hold college and advanced degrees. At East Liberty Church, however, I could see how very unwelcome and marginalized that could make someone feel who had not finished high school. And how do you lead new-member classes that might include folks with higher degrees on the one hand, and those who struggle to read or write on the other hand?

5

The challenges of diversity kept stretching me over the years of my ministry at East Liberty. Close encounters with those whose life experiences and circumstances differed so much from my own pushed me hard to rethink and reconfigure. Fortunately, I had help. Help came first and foremost from a God who had over the years kept nudging me out of my ruts. Good help came too from church staff and members who patiently assisted and supported me along the path. From my own experience at East Liberty I am convinced that the path leading toward our willingness to learn from those who differ from us, to grow our churches more deeply and widely into diversity, will also require that we ourselves simultaneously grow deeper and wider in our spirituality.

To grow wider in diversity, we must grow deeper spiritually because we will find our own preferences and prejudices stretched and challenged. We will be pushed toward a self-transcendence that leads us to ask why our own preferences in worship and music styles, for example, should routinely prevail over the preferences of neighbors from different social classes and cultures. We will have to ask ourselves, "Is there really anything inherent in my own likes and dislikes in church life that places me any closer than others to the essence of the Christian faith and life?"

In one important respect, the first congregation I served, from 1962 to 1966, helped to prepare me for the last congregation I would serve. These were heady and sometimes frightening days—the early years of the civil rights movement; the war on poverty; Vatican II; the assassination of JFK; a Republican turn to the far right with their nomination of Senator Barry Goldwater to oppose LBJ in the presidential election of 1964; the beginnings of the Vietnam War. From the pulpit I spoke against the paranoid, conspiratorial hysteria fostered by the likes of the Rev. Billy James Hargis's virulently anti-Communist Christian Crusade, the John Birch Society, and Goldwater's dictum that "extremism in the defense of liberty is no vice." I began my ministry in these tumultuous times, a rather outspoken young liberal fresh out of Harvard Divinity, serving a somewhat conservative, mostly blue-collar congregation in the exurban boondocks east of Cincinnati.

Calvin Presbyterian Church was a close-knit, loving congregation that somehow accepted and supported their young pastor no matter, it seemed, what he said or did—inviting a black pastor and a Catholic layman to the pulpit, joining in civil rights marches, challenging right-wing extremism and fundamentalism, or defending LBJ's war on poverty. Even when they disagreed with me, church members and leaders supported my pastoral/

prophetic right and responsibility to take the stands I felt called to advocate. In those years we learned together the possibility of forming close and loving relationships with folks whose views sometimes differed widely from our own, of being able to discuss those differences honestly and openly with mutual respect and affection. Some years later, in yet another congregation, I would learn from a former pastor the watchword, "Let us agree to disagree agreeably." But already at Calvin Church I had experienced the possibility of doing so with love.

Blessed be the ties that can bind our hearts in Christian love . . . even when we may otherwise be poles apart on matters about which we have deep convictions. One set of loving ties formed at Calvin Church more than half a century ago remains to this day. A politically conservative middle-aged couple with four teenagers drew Jan and me into their family circle, often having us to their home for after-church Sunday dinners, plying us with whiskey sours, challenging us to ping-pong matches, and drawing us into challenging but loving and respectful discussion about issues of the time.

Elder John Wiseman, civil engineer, thoughtful student of the Bible, conservative Republican, theological moderate, was the gentle "father who knows best" in this family. He chaired the pastoral search committee that brought us to Calvin Church. John and Jane Wiseman's fifteen-year-old son David, who was a youth member of that search committee, would go on to enter the ministry and is now retired following forty-plus years of faithful service to local congregations and three years of mission work in Guatemala. Over all these years we have continued to keep in touch, visiting back and forth between our home in Richmond and David and Jeannene's home in Cary, North Carolina. In the summer of 2016 Jane Wiseman, still in Cincinnati, celebrated her 100th birthday!

As we were leaving our first congregation, returning to Harvard for Ph.D. studies in 1966, John Wiseman wrote a beautiful tribute to our ministry at Calvin Church entitled "Footprints of a Pastor." Published by Harvard Divinity School and distributed to all alumni, it appears as an appendix in this book. I value it even more because, on some big questions of the day, the dear, good man who wrote it and I found ourselves in real disagreement. Blest be the ties that bind our hearts in Christian love!

CHAPTER 1

Getting to Both/And

IN 1942 THE CONSERVATIVE Party of Canada changed its name to the Progressive Conservative Party. At the time, a Canadian paper editorialized under the tongue-in-cheek banner "The Progressive Conservatives . . . or How to Move Forward Backward." It's amusing, of course, because the label seems so self-contradictory, so oxymoronic. But maybe it *is* possible to move forward backward. Many of us believe that, with Vatican II in the early 1960s, the Roman Catholic Church moved forward by moving backward to recapture some fundamental insights from the Protestant Reformation of the sixteenth century, as well as by embracing contributions of a tradition of historical-critical Protestant biblical scholarship that stretches back into the nineteenth century. Protestants, for their part, have moved forward in recent decades by moving backward to recapture the wisdom of medieval Catholic mystics, undertaking monastic retreats, singing chants from the ecumenical monastic community of Taizé in France, making pilgrimages, and walking labyrinths. Theologically, I believe, many us would consider ourselves either progressive conservatives or conservative progressives.

Christianity reveals paradox. Christianity, in fact, revels in paradox. Christianity offers us the mystery and complexity of *both/and* rather than the simplicity of *either/or*. Jesus Christ is *both* fully human *and* fully divine. He is *both* the Jesus of history *and* the Christ of faith. He is *both* Messiah/ King *and* suffering servant. His cross is *both* a death/defeat *and* a victory/ triumph. God is *both* three *and* one.

The Bible is filled with contradictions and paradoxes. Again and again it offers both good news and bad news, both severe warnings and gracious promises. Sometimes bad news is recast as good news. Consider the beatitudes. Aren't these paradoxical blessings? Blessed are the poor. Blessed are those who mourn, who are persecuted.

The same Jesus who talked about the narrow gate that leads to salvation and warned that few would enter therein—that same Jesus also teaches us of God's loving compassion for the lost and straying. So, he says, there is more rejoicing in heaven over one redeemed sinner than ninety-nine righteous ones (Luke 15:7).

How can it possibly make any sense to talk about God in such conflicting ways? How can Jesus paint a picture of a God who lays upon us nearly impossible demands of commitment and self-sacrifice, even telling us that we must aim for perfection, and then turn right around and tell us that this same God comes after us in a loving search-and-rescue mission when we are lost and straying—loving us, forgiving us, rejoicing in our being found when we have no right at all to expect it?

In his book on Thomas Merton, Henri Nouwen noted that Merton, the renowned Trappist monk, contemplative, and author, was also inclined to self-contradiction. In the introduction to one of his books, Merton warned his readers not to take each of his strong statements at face value, but to counterbalance each one with another equally strong statement to be found elsewhere in the same book. Merton believed that an appreciation of paradox and contradiction leads to an encounter with a truth beyond the power of logic and rationality to comprehend. He wrote:

> Life is a continual development . . . What is impossible today may suddenly become possible tomorrow. What is good and pleasant today may, tomorrow, become evil and odious. What seems right from one point of view may, when seem from a different aspect, manifest itself as completely wrong.[1]

But Jesus seems to have had something even more profound in mind. His little stories of the shepherd who goes in search of his one lost sheep out of a hundred, of the woman who diligently searches for her one lost coin—these are fundamental to Jesus's vision of God, of the Divine, of Ultimate Reality (Luke 15:1–10). These are not merely engaging little stories or notions in the mind of Jesus. No, Jesus lived this vision of God, a vision he embodied as he sought out and embraced lost and rejected ones.

The Gospel writers have Jesus telling stories like these to opponents who appear very good at either/or thinking. For them you are either

---

1. Quoted in Nouwen, *Thomas Merton*, 73.

righteous or unrighteous—and the righteous are to have nothing to do with the unrighteous. Jesus is, therefore, highly suspect in their view. They constantly object that he befriends the likes of tax collectors and sinners of all stripes.

Perhaps Jesus understood what modern psychology has helped us to comprehend anew—that we often project onto others the lost and rejected dark sides of our own inner depths. So pious, righteous, moralistic, uptight folk cannot tolerate these wayward folk because they represent a lost dimension in the lives of those who are passing judgment—that part of the self that wants to be free and spontaneous, adventurous, risk-taking, unfettered by conformity to rules and conventions. At the same time, of course, Jesus recognized that the tax collectors and sinners were also truly lost. They had lost that part of themselves that could affirm and respect the necessity of moral order, social structure, or responsibility to God and neighbor.

This helps us understand why the God of both Hebrew and Christian Scriptures is so concerned with the lost, with the rebellious, with the stranger and alien, the opponent and the enemy. It is because these are lost parts of the whole, lost parts of our own selves—even, we might dare to say, lost parts of God's own self for whom God cares with a great and redemptive compassion. God's aim is the restoration of wholeness, *shalom*, at-one-ment.

God calls us not only to care for our own kind, not just to concentrate all our energies on those with whom we feel most comfortable, compatible, in agreement. It is those with whom we feel at odds, those who seem to challenge and threaten us, those who seem foreign and alien to us—it is they from whom we may sometimes have the most to learn and to gain, and to whom we, in turn, may have the most to offer. When we make the movement from an *either/or* thinking to a *both/and* thinking, we can extend to one another the joyful promise of a heavenly wholeness.

These insights about the reconciliation of opposites and the healing of conflicts also speak to our own individual inner struggles. The movement toward wholeness in our interpersonal relations first begins within our own psyches. Jesus witnesses that it is not a simple matter of dividing up people between those who are lost and those who are not. Each of us has elements of lostness within ourselves, ways in which we have strayed and wandered. Each of us is both the searching woman and the lost coin. Jesus tells us that God cares so much and with such compassion that when a part of us is lost, it is as if a part of God is lost. Therefore, we ought also to care about the lost parts of our own selves.

In 1975 I took a step toward recovering what felt like a lost part of my self. After eleven years of higher education leading to a PhD from Harvard, and another five years serving on the faculty of McCormick Theological Seminary in Chicago, plus bouts of depression and years of psychotherapy along the way, I decided to leave academia. Slowly a realization had grown within me that I was not where I was meant to be, not doing what I was meant to do. Important parts of me were in danger of being lost, neglected, and rejected. I was not the whole self I longed to be.

Through all those years of higher education, a once-valued side of me had been neglected in favor of one-sided intellectual development. But now I realized anew that I had spiritual gifts, including a gift for empathy, a calling to weep with those who weep and rejoice with those who rejoice. The students in my McCormick advisory group confirmed this when, as I was leaving my position there in 1975, they presented me with a hand-made banner that I cherish to this day. It bears these words: ""You honored the truth of each person—our pains and our possibilities. Thank you."

Having once experienced the satisfactions of local church ministry during a four-year "break" between my Master of Divinity and PhD studies, nine years later I was now coming to see that it was in the parish that I felt most truly fulfilled. It was there that the wholeness of *both* my heart *and* my mind could best be employed. At age 36, the call to pastoral ministry that I first heard at age fifteen was calling me once again.

The call was to a congregation in my home state of Oklahoma, First Presbyterian Church of Norman. A town-and-gown congregation adjacent to the University of Oklahoma, it offered me a situation where my academic background and intellectual bent were relevant and appreciated. Somewhat surprisingly, perhaps, it was probably the most theologically liberal congregation I ever served, one where I took some flack, for example, for introducing the Apostles' Creed into the worship service. I struggled at times during my four years there with an entrenched "liberal" old guard in the church that also resisted my efforts to build friendlier relations with the other, more evangelical, Presbyterian church in town. Still, never over the next three decades until my retirement did I ever look back with regret or question the validity of my "re-call" to parish ministry.

In chapters 10 and 11, I will revisit this story of personal wholeness gained and regained, exploring it in the context of Christocentric mysticism and of our Christian calling to join, again and again, in "the Paschal mystery," dying and rising with Christ.

Where might God be calling us all today toward greater wholeness in the midst of our society's wider and deeper political and religious polarizations, a time of bitter divisiveness unknown since the Vietnam War? Dare we hope to make at least a modest contribution to healing by suggesting how faithful Christians can build bridges toward the center, how we might be progressive conservatives or conservative progressives? There is today, in fact, a growing movement of those who gladly claim the label "progressive evangelical." A Google search of that term or "evangelical liberal" will turn up any number of related blogs with thoughtful, open-minded exploration of these issues from the evangelical side. On one of them, Doug Pagitt has written:

> Progressive evangelicals have reevaluated our stances on many issues, such as including all people in our communities and lives, understanding economics and how our financial structures affect the poorest in the world, looking at the way we live and reconnect with the earth, realizing the harm human beings are doing to it, and discovering more responsible, regenerative ways of life in it.[2]

Jim Wallis and Ron Sider, of course, have long led the way toward a progressive evangelicalism that affirms the importance of justice-seeking and peacemaking in the life of Christian discipleship. Beyond that, however, some evangelicals have been demonstrating an amazing openness to rethink and revise doctrines like penal substitutionary atonement, and even purgatory and universal salvation.[3] The famous Anglican evangelical John Stott has declared: "Emotionally, I find the concept [of eternal torment] intolerable and do not understand how people can live with it without either cauterizing their feelings or cracking under the strain."[4]

Is a comparable development possible from the progressive side? Can progressives match the evangelical willingness that Pagitt affirms to reevaluate "our stances on many issues"? Can progressives reevaluate their

2. Pagett, "10 Things I Wish Everyone Knew."

3. On the atonement see, for example, Flood, *Healing the Gospel*. While Bell, *Love Wins*, is by far the best known of sympathetic evangelical considerations of the possibility of universal salvation, it is by no means one of a kind. Under the pseudonym of George MacDonald, Robin Parry published *The Evangelical Universalist* in 2004. Outstanding on the subject of purgatory is Walls, *Purgatory*.

4. Quoted in Allison, *Night Comes*, 100.

inclination to push the envelope of traditional, classical Christian faith so hard and far that at points it threatens to burst the seams of faith, hope, and love within our faith communities? Might our congregations themselves become crucibles for exploring and healing conflicts, for reconciling some of our theological, social, and political opposites?

I know very well that this is much easier said than done. I myself am often of two minds, which I struggle to reconcile. Yes, pastors are called, I believe, to be pastoral, to be reconcilers and peacemakers. But I also strongly believe that we are called to be prophets, to speak out, to advocate and to take a stand, sometimes even becoming activists for difficult, controversial causes of justice and peace and human well-being. Is it possible to be a pastoral prophet or a prophetic pastor? Is it possible *both* to take a strong stand on issues that divide people—*and*, at the same time, to work toward uniting people? With the election of Donald Trump as president, this is truly now a most urgent question for religious leaders, for people of faith, and for all people of good faith.

In planning adult educational offerings and sermons, I have found it makes a difference when a pastor expresses trust in a congregation's maturity and wisdom to handle tough topics of the day in Christian love, with open-mindedness and mutual respect. It can be helpful to offer workshops from time to time on the constructive handling of conflict and disagreements. We can, as Pastor Janet James has done at our Gayton Kirk here in Richmond, encourage parishioners with differing viewpoints to meet over coffee or lunch and listen with care to one another. We can teach listening skills and foster the spiritual disciplines that move us toward the kind of extraordinary empathy and compassion Jesus taught, loving enemies and praying for those who abuse us. We can actively support and encourage our communities to claim the maturity that is required to speak the truth in love, to work toward common understanding— and, when we fail, to agree to disagree agreeably.

My own practice over the years, when taking potentially controversial stands from the pulpit, has been to explain that in our Reformed tradition it is considered a part of the pastor's responsibility to do so; that I have studied our denomination's official positions on the issues in question; that I have sought to ground my own position in biblical and theological standards; and that I offer my views not as infallible dictums but, rather, as contributions to an ongoing dialogue in which my listeners are invited to participate. A sermon dialogue opportunity might be offered afterward.

Otherwise, I might extend an invitation such as this: "I've had my say now from the pulpit. If you want a turn to be heard, let me know and I'll treat you to lunch so I can listen to you and we can explore it further together."

It doesn't always work. Differences might be irreconcilable. We might agree to disagree agreeably, or we might not. Once in a sermon I recounted the true story of a young man who struggled with his homosexuality. He had been told by his pastor, his church, and his own family that his identity was unacceptable to them and to God. So he climbed a bridge and threw himself to his death. I commented, "No wonder there is a need for a group such as Fundamentalists Anonymous." Afterward, as I greeted worshippers at the church door, a woman looked me square in the eye and said, "You're inclusive of everyone but fundamentalists." I thought hard about that for some while afterward. How do we embrace those who would reject whole categories of "others"? This woman was a chief agitator for the rejection of an outstanding candidate for the position of music director in our church because he was gay. Part of the paradox is that an inclusive church is not for everyone. This is not to say that we intentionally want to rule anyone out. It is simply that if we profess an inclusive identity, not everyone will choose to identify with that, because it means including others whom they cannot accept. Sadly, some will choose to depart, to rule themselves out of a church that is aiming to welcome all.

Surely Jesus, fully human as he was, must have struggled with this too, and struggled hard with it. Yes, he is reported to have said, "Blessed are the peacemakers" (Matt 5:9). But he also said, "Do not think that I have come to bring peace to the earth; I have not come to bring peace, but a sword. . . one's foes will be members of one's own household" (Matt 10:34–45). He instructed his disciples that, if they entered a village where people were unwilling to listen to them, they should not waste their time. They were to shake the dust from their feet and move on (Matt 10:14; Luke 9:5; Mark 6:11).

Sometimes, sadly, we find that we are moving in such different universes from one another that there is really no ground for any reasonable dialogue. Sometimes one side or another may push matters to such unreasonable extremes that differences are irreconcilable and "divorce" is inevitable. From a faith perspective, when such a point is reached, when the very essence of the Christian faith seems at stake (traditionally designated as *status confessionis*), it may be necessary to take an uncompromising stand by issuing a Barmen Declaration in Nazi Germany, or a Belhar Confession in apartheid South Africa. Some now wonder if we are reaching such a time in American Christianity.

In their co-authored book, *The Meaning of Jesus,* Marcus Borg and N.T. Wright set an excellent example of how to engage in dialogue across conservative/progressive boundaries. Good friends and respected New Testament scholars who have come at their subject from very different places on the spectrum of issues about the historical Jesus, Borg and Wright have explored their differences with honesty and mutual respect.

Within the first year of Pope Francis's election, my son, R. Andrew Chesnut, the Bishop Walter Sullivan Chair of Catholic Studies at Virginia Commonwealth University, and I coauthored a piece on Andrew's *Huffington Post* blog entitled "Pope of Paradox." We noted Francis's tendency toward the reconciliation of opposites within himself and his ministry—not rejecting traditional church teachings, yet pastorally softening and reimagining them as something of a "compassionate conservative." We wrote:

> Looking to the new Pope's personal disposition and style, we might also call him "humbly assertive," or "a pastoral prophet." Francis goes out of his way to set himself alongside rather than above others, to be a good listener, collaborative rather than hierarchical and authoritarian. Yet he does not hesitate to state his own views on potentially controversial matters, as when asked what he thought about homosexual priests, he declared "Who am I to judge?" Coming from the supreme pontiff, that statement itself is an astonishing example of both humility and assertiveness . . .
>
> So Pope Francis professes a faith that affirms both/and rather than either/or. It is an attitude and a vision that can produce the most creative, innovative, problem-solving leadership. In this age of bitter political polarization and of violent religious extremism, Pope Francis offers us, it seems, exactly the sort of moderating, reconciling leadership that our divided world so sorely needs.[5]

Admittedly, Francis is disappointing to conservatives in many respects and to progressives in his positions on gay marriage and the place of women in the church. Still, overall, he offers a moderating, reconciling vision of leadership that points the way for us all. So these will also be our aims in the pages that follow: embracing paradox; being pastorally prophetic; striving to avoid divisiveness while speaking the truth in love; affirming both/and positions; and finding a faithful center. So help us God.

5. Chesnut and Chesnut, "Pope of Paradox."

CHAPTER 2

Progressive Christianity in the Desert

ABOUT THE SIZE OF Manhattan, Ghost Ranch in northern New Mexico is twenty-one thousand acres of high desert country dotted with sage brush and mesquite, juniper, and piñon pine. Tamarisk and cottonwood line the arroyos, while bluffs and mesas tower above, layered in red and yellow pastels, deep purples and sandy beiges. The conference grounds themselves are nestled in a lush green valley oasis surrounded by soaring rock formations whose breathtaking colors constantly change from dawn to dusk with the sunlight's shifting angles.

New Mexicans call their state "the land of enchantment." Nowhere is this more palpable than at Ghost Ranch. It is truly what the Celts have called a "thin place," where the boundary between heaven and earth feels porous, permeable. At night the brilliantly illuminated Milky Way can seem near enough to stir with your hand. (City dwellers, when was the last time you saw the Milky Way?) After dark it is not unusual to witness half a dozen or more deer silently grazing in the meadow that lies at the center of the ranch's complex of modest adobe buildings. Here also, occasionally, one may experience the very fiercest of desert thunderstorms that suddenly send towering, potentially destructive walls of water rushing down the ordinarily dry arroyos. Disconcerting, inconvenient, even frightening, this too strikes one as befitting the biblical nature of the place.

In 1955 Arthur and Phoebe Pack, who had operated it as a dude ranch, gave the Ghost Ranch property to the Presbyterian Church (PCUSA at the time). The ranch was an easy one-day drive from my western Oklahoma home, but 1955 was the year I graduated from high school and left for college in Ohio, so many years passed before I finally got there. Living east of the Mississippi for the next twenty years, it was 1977, when I was pastoring the First Presbyterian Church in Norman, Oklahoma, that I made my first visit to the ranch. Over the next decades my wife and I enjoyed many summer weeks at the ranch. Again and again, both taking and teaching courses there and finally serving on the board, we found spiritual refreshment at the ranch, nourishment and renewal to sustain the vision of a progressive faith that we have also sought to develop and nurture in the congregations we have served.

Envision the colorful, comprehensive collage of educational and re-creational experiences offered at Ghost Ranch. Every season there is a vast array of courses in the arts—watercolor and pottery, weaving and pastels, blacksmithing and jewelry making, singing, stained glass, paper art, photography. The renowned twentieth-century artist Georgia O'Keefe made the ranch her home for many decades and accomplished the bulk of her work here, with Ghost Ranch scenes providing her primary inspiration.

The ranch, which houses both archeological and paleontological museums, offers courses in these and other sciences—geology, land management, agriculture, ecology. This same land is also home to one of the top ten sites in the United States for the excavation of dinosaur bones. Here there is open acceptance of the compatibility between, on the one hand, faith in God the Creator and, on the other hand, recognition of scientific facts that point to the earth and life upon the earth having been created through natural forces requiring billions of years of evolutionary development. Just outside the ranch library (which for many years was voluntarily staffed by a retired head librarian from MIT) there stands a six-foot-tall column representing, layer by geological layer, the age of the earth. The topmost layer, merely paper thin, reflects the years of our human life on the planet.

The ranch curriculum also includes, of course, offerings in theology and spirituality, worship, social justice, and peacemaking. There are opportunities for labyrinth walking, hiking and horseback riding, camping, and star gazing. There are daily times for worship, spiritual direction, meditation, and massage, with hot springs and mud baths not far away. This is an amazingly open space spiritually. A large Sikh population, a Muslim commune, a Catholic monastery, and Native American communities are not far away. Interfaith interactions are frequent and respectfully explored. Courses on the future of the church were offered by gay leaders long before that would have been acceptable in many other places in church and society. Seekers and doubters have long found a hospitable welcome and a comfortable climate in which to raise their questions.

Celtic theologian John Phillip Newell, best known perhaps for his *Listening for the Heartbeat of God: A Celtic Spirituality,* has for many years now been the ranch's "Companion Theologian." It is a particularly fitting association with an author and teacher who draws upon traditions that affirm the sacramental presence of the divine within the world of nature, honoring the reality of "thin places" like Ghost Ranch. Since the early 2000s Newell, his wife Alison, and other spiritual guides have had at their disposal a residence known as Casa del Sol, a renovated old adobe ranch house now serving as a quiet, remote residence for spiritual retreatants.

Ghost Ranch has also long embodied a socially responsible Christian faith. Sustainable land management and agriculture are practiced. With extensive rural poverty in the area, Ghost Ranch has striven, in various ways, to be a good neighbor. Area schoolchildren are welcomed, free of charge, to the museum. Free swimming lessons are given. Local artists and artisans are offered a venue for selling their creations. Several years back, Ghost Ranch leaders were instrumental in assisting the area's Hispanic landowners to finally obtain land titles that had been in legal limbo ever since the United States took the territory from Mexico in the war of 1846–48.

Days spent at Ghost Ranch helped to sustain Jan and me in some rough times when, for a couple of years in the second half of the 1990s, our Pittsburgh church endured some rather intense theological struggles. It was then that a cadre of more-conservative members challenged Jan (who was then responsible for adult education) for inviting Professor Susan Nelson, from nearby Pittsburgh Theological Seminary and a Parish Associate at our church, to offer a course on feminist theology. I made these folks unhappy by proposing that we host theologian Matthew Fox of creation spirituality fame, by exploring with an open mind themes of New Age belief in sermons and adult classes, and by advocating for the welcome both of LGBT folk and of seekers with more questions than answers about their faith. Our new labyrinth ministry, they alleged, was really "pagan." Our mid-week Taizé service, they said, was "crypto-Catholic."

Returning to Pittsburgh from a time of spiritual refreshment in the Ghost Ranch desert in the summer of 1998, Jan and I came home more convinced than ever that we were on the right track with our Pittsburgh church. Like Elijah emerging from his high desert cave, we had been reminded at the ranch that we were not alone. Once again we were reassured that a vital, dynamic, progressive Christian faith was alive and well. As always before, at Ghost Ranch we were renewed in an open-minded, open-hearted Christianity that trusts the truth, whatever its source, wherever it leads. Here was a kind of Christianity that trusts the God of the whole universe and of all people. I believe this is progressive Christianity at its best: a Christianity that is not afraid of science, nor of human creativity and the arts, nor of other faiths and spiritual traditions, nor of spiritual seekers and their questions, nor of humankind's God-given differences of culture or personality or sexual/gender identity, nor of the sacramentality of nature in the thin places it provides, nor of false accusations of nature worship, pantheism, or syncretism.

However, in fairness to those in our congregation who harbored strong suspicions about the progressive directions of our ministry, it is also right to recognize the validity of some of their concerns. One of our most persistent critics (a young woman whose father was a Southern Baptist minister) once challenged me concerning all the newcomers we were welcoming—people who, in her opinion, "really don't know what they believe." And, she demanded of me, "What do *we* really believe? What is our core?"

It was a fair question. The desert, as well as being a place for spiritual sustenance and renewal, can also be a place for losing one's bearings, for getting dangerously disoriented and hopelessly lost. Tragically, this happened in 1969 to the late Episcopalian Bishop James Pike, who died in the desert of Israel as he and his third wife, on a personal and somewhat quixotic quest for the historical Jesus, searched for the ancient Qumran community. Many might say—at least by their own core standards of Christian belief—that progressive, skeptical James Pike had sadly lost his bearings long before he died in the Judean desert. Many would say the same about certain expressions of progressive Christianity today.

Deborah Smith Douglas, in a recent review of John Phillip Newell's new book, *The Rebirth of God*, has said very nearly as much about his latest effort:

> Newell doesn't really seem to care much about Christianity. Little in these pages indicates awareness or exploration of current problems facing the church at any level. On the other hand, Newell seems greatly concerned to suggest only remedies that would be inoffensive to Jewish, Buddhist, Hindu, or even spiritual-but-not-religious New Age readers.

The attempt to be inclusive renders the solutions anodyne—of the least-common-denominator variety rather than anything reflective of distinctively Christian theology or practice. References to Jesus are thin on the ground, and New Testament citations are few; when Newell does use them, he almost always dilutes them or generalizes them into oblivion. For instance, "the story of the incarnate Christ" is not a scandalous particularity, the deepest of sacred mysteries. Instead, it merely "points to the oneness of . . . spirit and matter," revealing "the sacredness of every person."

A clue to Newell's reluctance to use language that is unequivocally Christian is his repeated use of the title image of "rebirthing God." As the death and resurrection of Jesus are indispensable to Christian theology and differentiate Christianity from other religions, Newell seems to have found it easier to avoid dying-and-rising language and instead to speak in vaguely animist or Hindu terms of rebirth.[1]

Personally, this hurts. From our years in Santa Fe my wife and I know both Douglas and Newell. We respect and admire them and their contributions. We have made extensive use of Newell's *Listening for the Heartbeat of God* in classes we have taught. His Ghost Ranch workshops and devotional writings have enriched our spiritual life. Considering the whole of his work, in particular his *New Harmony*, in which he forthrightly confesses our tragic human brokenness and affirms the centrality of Christ and his loving sacrifice for the healing of the world, I would rise to Newell's defense.

Still, Douglas's stinging critique deserves to be taken seriously. I am inclined to believe that she would surely offer similar judgments were she to review David Felten and Jeff Procter-Murphy's *Living the Questions: The Wisdom of Progressive Christianity*, a book advertised by the publisher as "the most comprehensive, indeed, the only survey of progressive Christianity in existence today."[2] If indictments such as Douglas's are more broadly true of progressive Christianity today, it is right to ask if it retains anything distinctively Christian. Or is it simply lost in the desert, dangerously wandering without bearings? Living the questions of faith is all well and good, but mustn't we have some answers to proffer that are more than "anodyne . . . of the least-common-denominator variety"?

1. Douglas, "Rebirthing," 41.

2. https://www.amazon.com/Living-Questions-Wisdom-Progressive-Christianity/dp/0062109367.

What is our core? It's a fair question, an essential question. Is there a progressive Christian faith that can answer this question in a distinctively *Christian* way, while still qualifying as *progressive*? This is one of the searchlight questions that will guide our explorations in the pages to follow. And yes, as we shall see, I did have a ready answer for that conservative young woman who challenged my progressive inclinations by asking me about the core of our faith.

CHAPTER 3

The Big-Picture Bible
—a Progressive View

SO MANY OF THE differences and disagreements among Christians—left, right, and center—arise from the different ways we read the Bible. Since the Bible is such a large and diverse collection of various types of literature, written by individually unique authors, each with personal and cultural points of view and together representing a span of almost a millennium and a half, different readers will come to different conclusions when it comes to deciding where the Bible as a whole comes down on some of the big questions. On a particular issue such as gender equality, for example, Jesus can be seen as having one perspective, Paul another. More conservative Christians tend to favor the patriarchal sources; progressives prefer the more egalitarian witnesses. It seems we might have a better chance of resolving many of our differences, of moving toward common ground, if we had some overarching frame of reference, some means of sorting out the basics and essentials.

Perhaps, like me, you had your own special childhood Bible. Mine was an oversized book with large print and big pictures—"a big picture Bible." I distinctly remember, as a preschooler, seeing there for the very first time a drawing of Jesus hanging on the cross. That picture made an indelible impression on my heart and mind, one that will remain with me until my own dying day.

What is the big picture Bible you carry in your head? What stories and verses and messages and principles stand out above the rest? Is it Moses and the Exodus? David and Goliath? Jonah and the whale? The twenty-third

Psalm? The nativity story? The Golden Rule? The crucifixion and resurrection of Christ? Paul's verses about love in 1 Corinthians 13?

Because the Bible, in all its great scope and diversity, is a complex collection of at least sixty-six different documents, we can neither make much sense of it, nor make much consistent good use of it, unless we recognize (1) that it requires interpretation, and (2) that in order to interpret it we must have some big-picture concept of what matters most in it, of what its overarching themes and consistent messages are. Otherwise, how do we sort out what is the eternally enduring word of God from what are the very human, fallible viewpoints of its various and diverse human authors?

Much of the teaching of Jesus can be understood as an effort to move the people of his time—especially the religious leaders and interpreters of faith—to focus on the big picture of the Hebrew tradition. This is exactly the point he was making when he said: "Woe to you, scribes and Pharisees, hypocrites! For you tithe mint, dill, and cumin, and have neglected the weightier matters of the law: justice and mercy and faith. . . . You strain out a gnat but swallow a camel!" (Matt 23:23–24). In other words, said Jesus, you can't see the forest for the trees. You can't see the big picture. The big picture, said Jesus, is to love God with all your heart, mind, soul, and strength, and your neighbor as yourself (Mark 12:28–31; Matt 22:36–40). This, he said, is the essence, or the big picture, of the law and prophets. The big picture is fairness, justice, kindness, mercy, and compassion. The big picture is doing unto others as you would have them do unto you (Matt 7:12; Luke 6:31). The big picture, as the prophet Micah said long before, is to do justice, and love kindness, and walk humbly with your God (Micah 6:8). Without the big picture in mind, the kind of religion that we can end up with—in the first century and in our own time of rigid, resurgent fundamentalisms (not only within Christianity, of course, but within other religions as well)—is a faith that abandons the big picture of the scriptures for a faith that is its antithesis, a faith of intolerance and exclusion. So we get religions that, as Jesus said of his legalistic opponents, lay heavy burdens on people, blocking the path that leads into God's kingdom (Matt 23:4, 13) rather than welcoming people into an abundant life in God's realm of mercy and fairness for all.

In the spring of 1962, as I was approaching graduation from Harvard Divinity School and seeking a call to ministry, I corresponded with churches seeking a pastor. One congregation in my home state of Oklahoma responded to my initial inquiry with two questions: (1) Did I smoke? (2) Did

I believe that Jonah was actually swallowed by the whale? Smoking was apparently their litmus test for living a Christian life. And a literal reading of Jonah was their litmus test for correct biblical interpretation.

Actually, I believe Jonah does provide a very good litmus test of how we either find or obscure the big picture of the Bible, even within just this one short book. After all, what do most church people likely remember from Sunday school about the story of Jonah? Isn't it the supposed miracle of Jonah being swallowed alive but then surviving three days in the belly of that great fish (It is not a "whale" in the biblical account)?

But the real miracle in the Jonah story is its teaching—centuries before Jesus—that God loves our most hated and feared enemies, calling us to have the same transcendent care that God has for the fate of all people. Jonah, you see, was a reluctant messenger of God's mercy. He was fleeing the call to be God's agent in saving from destruction the people of Nineveh, capital of Assyria, the dreaded and despised foes of Jonah's own Jewish people. Thus it was in his flight from God's call that Jonah got caught up in the belly of the great fish and then eventually redirected to help save Nineveh.

The book of Jonah and the words of Jesus come to us centuries apart with the same message, a message that surely must be a key element within our big picture Bible: a message to love our enemies. That's a lot harder to swallow than any big fish story! Maybe I should have responded to that Oklahoma church by telling them I would answer *their* question about Jonah if they would answer *my* question about Jonah: Do you really believe the story's message?

The essential message of Jonah has nothing to do with whether or not the events of the story actually took place—no more so than whether or not Jesus's parable of the Good Samaritan is about events that actually took place. Focusing on literal historicity here is a distraction, and a dangerous one, because it let us off the hook by taking our focus away from the core message of the story. It is only in the message of both stories that we find the word of God, the enduring, eternal truth.

We must come to the Bible with appropriate expectations and read it in appropriate ways. Otherwise we risk turning the Bible into something it is not: a legalistic code book that provides comprehensive and infallible answers to every moral dilemma of our own time, or a scientific account of exactly how the earth was formed, or an objective historical record of events that actually took place in every detail as reported, or a soothsayer's guidebook predicting every stage of the future and exactly how and when the world will end.

All of these assumptions about the Bible may, when applied, produce distorting, even dangerous distractions from the scripture's big-picture messages. Mistaken readings of the Bible can make it into a tool of prejudice and oppression, just as it was used in the past to support holy war and slavery. So a crucial question that we ought to ask ourselves is this: Is the way I read the Bible and understand its message and authority today compatible or incompatible with the interpretive approach of those in the past—including many to this very day—whose Bible is taken to justify racism, second-class status for women, or condemnation for and discrimination against those of differing sexual identities?

What is the positive content of this big-picture Bible of which we speak? In a very real way, it is the central task of this volume to answer that question. In my own faith tradition, we affirm that the Bible's authority as the word of God (with a small "w") derives from its witness to Jesus Christ as the living Word of God. We see the big picture through a Christ-centered focus (affirming all the while how very rooted Jesus was in his own Hebrew Scriptures), from his work and word and witness. Much of our attention throughout these pages, therefore, will be given to drawing out the big picture that we derive in and through Jesus, the Christ. What was most important to him? For example, what does it suggest to us about the relative importance of sexuality versus wealth and material possession when we consider that Jesus gave far more attention to the latter than to the former as he talked about faithful living?

The task of biblical interpretation will also, however, carry us beyond the Bible itself. As we struggle to make sense in our own time and place of writings that emerged in ever-changing worlds with ever-shifting cultural contexts, we will inevitably find ourselves engaging in theological reflection. If we formulate our understanding of a big-picture faith using John Wesley's "quadrilateral" method for working out those faith formulations, I believe we will have better success than by trying to follow the Protestant reformers' "*sola scriptura*," or at least the narrow way in which some would interpret *sola scriptura*. Wesley's formula for using scripture, tradition, experience and reason identifies the framework within which any biblical interpretation, any theological reflection, must proceed if we are not to capitulate to biblicism, the notion that a literal reading of scripture is all we really need to make good sense of our faith. The reformers, of course, drew upon the tradition of early church fathers and creeds. Reason and experience open us to the findings of science about the age of the earth, climate change, the structure of the cosmos, and the nature of human sexuality. Our own life experiences, as the personal portions of this book aim to illustrate, can open us to new insights and understandings of the enduring truths of scripture and tradition.

At the same time, we must acknowledge that the problem of a literal biblical historicism lies not only at the conservative end of the theological spectrum. We find something like it on the progressive side as well—especially among those who follow the "Jesus Seminar" of ultra-skeptical scholars whose sometimes reductionist search for the historical Jesus would strip away whatever in the gospel accounts does not measure up to their own preconceptions about what could or could not have been "historical." For example, why should we not assume that which many who identify with the Jesus Seminar would deny—that Jesus had some notion of how it might all end for himself? Did Jesus have no sense that he might finally be called to offer his life in martyrdom, or even as a vicarious redeeming sacrifice? Why should we not assume that Jesus's own sense of his calling might have evolved over time and that we can, therefore, expect to find some evidence of a progressive development of his self-understanding within the Gospel records? Why should we expect all of his teachings to be consistent with one another, to reflect no development or struggle or even contradiction?

In my freshman Bible courses at the College of Wooster I learned to appreciate an understanding of the revelation of God as a progressive movement over time. In the Hebrew Scriptures, for example, we see a development away from an earlier harsh, punitive, ethnocentric, even genocidal understanding of God and God's will as displayed in stories of the conquest of Canaan. Eventually the progression takes us toward prophets such as Isaiah, Hosea, and Jonah with their affirmations of a much more compassionate, inclusive, universal God of all peoples.

I think it also makes good sense to affirm the possibility of a progression of understanding within the views of Jesus himself. Here I am indebted to the insight of Dr. Charles W. Brockwell, Jr., my good friend stretching back to our student days at Harvard Divinity School, beginning in 1959. Brockwell reasons that Jesus himself began his ministry closer to John the Baptist, with a stricter, harsher message about entering God's impending Kingdom, but then moved toward a more compassionate, pastoral approach as his heart was moved by seeing the needy crowds flock to him as sheep without a shepherd (Matt 9:36). Indeed, we can see exactly such a movement in the remarkable story of Jesus's encounter with a Canaanite woman (Matt 15:21–28; cf. the Syrophoencian woman in Mark 7). Outspoken, assertive, she apparently managed in one brief moment to shift Jesus away from a harsh, narrow focus on ministering only to Jews toward responding to the needs of others who were outside that tight, exclusive circle.

A skeptical New Testament scholar such as Bart Ehrman concludes that even though Jesus might well have understood himself to be the Messiah, he did not foresee that his own untimely death might be part of that calling. But why must we assume that it was only the Gospel writers who were responsible, decades later, for putting together that extraordinary, seemingly contradictory combination of two very different figures in the Hebrew scriptures—the kingly Messiah on the one hand and the suffering servant of Isaiah on the other hand?

Couldn't the creative, paradoxical reconciliation of these two seemingly opposite roles—the kingly Messiah and the vicariously suffering servant —have occurred to Jesus himself as he began to see and ponder how things were unfolding toward the end of his ministry? In fact, in later chapters we will consider the possibility that Jesus might have appropriated from an already long-established Jewish tradition the notion of a suffering, redeeming divine Messiah. But for now let us assume that Luke is right: that at the very start of his ministry Jesus drew his own mission statement from Isaiah's mission statement of the servant of the Lord (Luke 4:18–19). Surely it would not then be unlikely that Jesus might also, toward the end of his ministry, have drawn upon Isaiah's mission statement of the suffering servant of the Lord to understand how it was all unfolding for him:

> Surely he has borne our infirmities and carried our diseases . . . But he was wounded for our transgressions, crushed for our iniquities; upon him was the punishment that made us whole, and by his bruises we are healed. (Isa 53:4–5)

Still, even if Jesus did begin to conclude that he might be uniquely called as a suffering, dying sort of servant Messiah, he also understandably could have harbored significant doubts and uncertainties about it all. What sense could it make? How on earth could it possibly conclude? Thus on his last night of anguish, he cried out to God that this "cup" of suffering might pass from him, but also, nevertheless, that in the end God's will should be done (Matt 26:39). So finally, on the cross, he cried out in doubt and despair, asking why God had forsaken him (Matt 27:46; Mark 15:34).

Even if we accept, with many skeptical New Testament scholars, that the Jesus of history could not by the time of his death have seen any clear light at the end of the tunnel that might have enabled him to make sense of it all, certainly the post-resurrection disciples could see what Jesus himself might not have fully seen. These earliest witnesses and believers could and did begin to put it all together, their unfolding big picture of the Jesus story. This is why their accounts, not just the bare bones of a conjectured historical Jesus, must be foundational for our own faith. Yes, surely, those who affirm the full humanity of Jesus can also affirm that the meaning of his story would have progressively developed within Jesus's own mind during his days on earth. Then, of course, the sacred story continued to develop after his death and resurrection. So those who bore earliest witness to it all and came to understand it possibly more fully than even Jesus himself was able to while it was still unfolding through him and around him—they too must be a big part of our own big-picture Bible. As New Testament scholar Dale Allison has put it:

> If I may . . . use the language of Paul, Jesus became a life-giving spirit, who moved into the early Christians and their texts, with their memories and their fictions, their speculations and their debates. Jesus' life reached beyond itself, to live on in others. If we ignore them, don't we ignore him?[1]

As we seek to understand who Jesus was and what he taught, Allison offers a very sensible approach. Unlike the Jesus Seminar scholars, who try to evaluate verse by verse what Jesus actually did or did not say, often on the basis of rather subjective standards and preconceptions, Allison suggests we look for the big-picture Jesus:

> Given that we typically remember the outlines of an event or the general purport of a conversation rather than the particulars and that we extract patterns and meaning from our memories, it makes little sense to open the quest for Jesus by evaluating individual items with our criteria, in the hope that some bits preserve pristine memory. We should rather be looking for repeating patterns and contemplating the big picture.
>
> With regard to the sources for Jesus, the traditional criteria of authenticity privilege the parts over the whole. It seems more

1. Allison, *Historical Christ*, Chapter 1.

prudent to privilege generalizations drawn from the whole than to concentrate upon one individual item after another.[2]

So, to cite some key examples, when we follow Allison's approach, the big-picture Jesus clearly comes across as a miracle worker/healer, as proclaimer of an eschatological message of God's imminent Kingdom, and, in fact, as the one sent by God to play the leading role in ushering in those end times. But all of this, significant as it is, is only part of the even bigger picture of the Jesus we will find in the pages to come.

2. Ibid., Chapter 3.

CHAPTER 4

Faith Matters

THE OLD TESTAMENT PROPHET Habakkuk was one very discouraged individual. His message begins with an anguished cry to God: How long, O Lord? How long must our land be plagued with violence, with greed and deprivation and injustice? How long must the wicked prosper and innocent people suffer? How long must we cry to you, O God, and get no answer, no relief, no help? (1:1–4, paraphrased)

Though it may seem strange to say, Habakkuk displays a kind of core faith that can embrace even the loss of faith, a faith that does not turn away from God in the midst of life's most serious questions and doubts, a faith that takes those questions and doubts directly to God. His, we might say, is the kind of faith that was "living the questions." This is the kind of astonishing faith that can say, with the father who took his boy to be healed by Jesus, "I believe; help my unbelief" (Mark 9:24). It is, if we may use the expression, the kind of "incredible faith" the world has witnessed during my own lifetime, faith that somehow has enabled faithful Jews to keep on believing even after the Holocaust. This is truly foundational faith, rock-bottom faith, a hardest-core kind of faith.

How does God answer Habakkuk? How does God respond to the prophet's complaints, his doubts, his challenges to God's justice and goodness? God responds, Habakkuk tells us, with a few good, brief words of reassurance and encouragement:

> Then the Lord answered me and said:
> "Write the vision;
>   make it plain on tablets,
> so that a runner may read it.

For there is still a vision for the appointed time;
it speaks of the end, and does not lie.
If it seems to tarry, wait for it;
it will surely come, it will not delay.
Look at the proud!
Their spirit is not right in them;
but the righteous live by their faith." (2:2–4)

God says, in essence: The vision I've given you is trustworthy. It will not fail. A better, more just, more peaceful world is coming. In the meantime, Habakkuk, hang in there. Keep the faith. Trust in God.

The righteous shall live by faith, God tells Habakkuk. This was, of course, one of Martin Luther's key verses, foundational for his doctrine of justification by faith through grace. This was the banner Luther held aloft, the reformation watchword. Luther stood over against the church's teachings at that time that we could earn our way into God's favor by doing good works, acts of penance, even monetary contributions. No, said Luther, God's favor is not something to be earned or bought and sold. It is God's free gift through God's saving work in Christ. You can claim that gift only by faith, by trust in God's grace, not in your own achievements.

What is faith? Again and again in his challenging book, *The Underground Church*, progressive United Church of Christ pastor Robin Meyers makes the point that faith is trust, not assent to creeds and doctrines. And that is the message we hear from Habakkuk. God is saying: Trust me, Habakkuk. Trust the vision I have given you of a better world, of peace and justice. Live by that vision. Live by your trust in that God-given vision. That is what Martin Luther was saying to Christians in his time: Trust in God's goodness and grace, not in yourself, not in your own acts of penance, church donations, good deeds, or righteousness.

So Robin Meyers is absolutely right when he insists that faith is not first and foremost about assent to propositions, doctrines, and creeds. At its heart and core, faith is trust. As the epistle of James says, "You believe that God is one; you do well. Even the devils believe and shudder" (2:19). In other words, if your faith is only belief, only assent to the proposition that God exists, that really doesn't amount to much. Even the devils believe that God exists. The real question is this: Is your life founded on trust in God? Does that trust, that allegiance, that devotion, shape who you are and how you live?

In *On God's Side*, Jim Wallis reflects on a debate he had with Al Mohler, president of Southern Baptist Theological Seminary:

> The theology that deals only with the atonement, one of personal salvation and the life hereafter, was the theology of both my Plymouth Brethren church and Al Mohler's Southern Baptist church. Both churches, mine and his, missed the greatest moral issue of our time. We missed the civil rights movement, and most of our white Christian brothers and sisters were on the wrong side of it. When a church gets something that big that wrong, it certainly raises very deep questions about its theology. The theology of our churches made the church complicit with white racism, opposed to the civil rights movement, and completely unsupportive of our brothers and sisters in the black church. That enormous moral failure drove me and many other young people away from the churches and faith of our childhoods.[1]

So much of evangelical Christianity in our time seems perilously close to severing the both/and link between faith and good works. Believing in Jesus as Savior threatens to displace trusting Jesus as Lord. The result can be what Dietrich Bonhoeffer characterized as "cheap grace" in his *Cost of Discipleship*, a work that profoundly influenced me in my seminary days and has ever since. Trusting Jesus as Lord requires honoring his teachings by actually following his teachings that we should care about the suffering of those who have been impoverished, victimized, oppressed, and discriminated against. So much emphasis can be placed on a doctrinaire, formulaic, reductionist understanding of salvation by grace *alone* through faith *alone* that good works—scorned as "works righteousness"—can be denigrated as an impediment to salvation. Well-known evangelical pastor and author Timothy Keller recently said in an interview with Nicholas Kristof of the *New York Times*, "Jesus' teaching was not the main point of his mission. He came to save people through his death for sin and his resurrection."[2] Doesn't this sound like, "Don't worry about his teachings; it's the doctrine that matters"? What becomes of "Follow me"? This kind of thinking may help us understand how so many supposedly devout, Bible-believing Christians could ignore troubling issues of character and morality, compassion and justice to support a candidate like Donald Trump.

1. Wallis, *On God's Side*, 242.
2. Kristof, "Am I a Christian?"

Jesus himself, however, could not have been clearer on this point. It is not those who cry "Lord, Lord," who will enter God's kingdom, but those who do the will of the Father. It is, instead, "by their fruits" that his true disciples will be known (Matt 7:16–21). It is those who have treated the sick, the hungry, the imprisoned, and the stranger as if they were Christ himself in need—it is they who will be welcomed into God's kingdom, not those who thought they could be his disciples without doing so. This will be the standard by which God's final judgment of nations and souls will be made (Matt 25:31–46).

It is too bad that Luther himself muddied the waters by dismissing James as an "epistle of straw." James is just as clear as Jesus about the importance of good works, and about the impotence of faith without works:

> What good is it, my brothers and sisters, if you say you have faith but do not have works? Can faith save you? If a brother or sister is naked and lacks daily food, and one of you says to them, "Go in peace; keep warm and eat your fill," yet you do not supply their bodily needs, what is the good of that? So faith by itself, if it has no works, is dead.
>
> But someone will say, "You have faith and I have works." Show me your faith apart from your works, and I by my works will show you my faith. (2:14–18)

However, I must take exception to Meyers and others when they go beyond claiming that faith is trust, by further asserting that *faith is not also belief*. I say that it is impossible to separate faith and belief. I say it is not *either/or*. I say it is *both/and*. So, yes, it is not enough just to believe that God exists. However, how can I trust in God unless I do first believe that God exists? And can I trust in God unless I also believe that God is good and trustworthy?

The propositions in which we believe do matter. Our beliefs do matter. Do I believe that only Christians can be saved and that everyone else is damned to hell? It matters. Do I believe that the world around us is God's good creation and that we are God's appointed stewards to take care of the environment? Or do I believe that the material world is there for humans to exploit in any way we choose for our own immediate gain? It matters. Do I believe that greed is good? Do I believe that society should be ordered around the principle of unfettered free enterprise, each one for himself and the devil take the hindmost? It matters.

Do I believe that God is a personal God of love with whom I can interact, a God I can question and challenge as Habakkuk did? Or do I believe that God is some sort of impersonal force to whom it would be senseless to pray or to put challenging questions? It matters. How can I possibly put my trust in an impersonal force? It does matter what I believe. What can we believe about human nature? What can we believe about the cross? About life after death, and heaven and hell? About the Bible? About the nature of faith itself? I believe that we must think about our faith. We must consider, examine, and reexamine what we believe and why.

Robin Meyers comes out of a tradition (the churches of Christ, in which he grew up, later switching to the Congregational side of the UCC) that has tended to eschew official creeds and doctrines. I come out of a tradition that honors creeds and doctrines and the discipline of theology. Robin Meyers thinks formulating and professing statements of faith will divide us. I think they can unite us. Developing formal statements of faith allows us to think through and formulate our faith in disciplined, communal ways, and then to profess and affirm our core identity as a Christian community.

It is very important to note, however, that in the Presbyterian tradition we do not regard our statements of faith as ever complete or final, absolute or written in stone. Presbyterians have whole books of faith statements, going back to the Apostles' and Nicene Creeds and up to the present time. We keep on reexamining and rethinking and restating what we believe, taking into account scripture, tradition, reason, and experience. Our faith is an evolving, dynamic, emerging, living thing, not dead and static. But then what if you disagree with the decisions that—through a democratic process of due deliberation and majority vote—the rest of us have reached about our faith? That's okay. We'll draw you into the discussion and keep on thinking about it, thinking together about what we believe and perhaps eventually reformulate it once again.

What is faith? Jesus gives us some important clues. Jesus said the two great commandments are to love God with all our heart, mind, soul, and strength, and to love our neighbors as ourselves. To love God with *all your heart* is to trust God, to respond to God's loving trustworthiness with your own loving trustworthiness. To love God with *all your mind* is to think about what you believe, to take seriously what you believe about serious matters such as the nature of God, the purpose of life, the purpose of *your* life. To love God with *all your soul* is to nurture your personal relationship with God through prayer and meditation and worship. To love God with *all your strength* is to demonstrate your faith by the way you live, by giving your time, effort, and energy to loving God by loving your neighbors. This is complete faith, whole faith.

One more ingredient in the biblical understanding of faith deserves to be highlighted, one that is closely linked to all the above yet carries us even further and deeper than belief or trust. New Testament scholar Michael Gorman, reflecting on the meaning of the root word for faith in Greek (*pist* as used in the writings of Paul), puts it this way in his *Becoming the Gospel: Paul, Participation, and Mission*:

> In Paul's world the *pist* word-family [i.e., the Greek word for faith] usually indicates faithfulness, and it has been suggested by a number of scholars that although this word-family is difficult to render into English, especially with one word, a phrase like "believing allegiance," "faithful allegiance," or "trusting loyalty" comes close to conveying its core meaning in many instances.[3]

For Paul, as Gorman makes abundantly clear, this means a faith that entails faithfulness even unto suffering and death.

Robin Meyers says that what we do as Christians is far more important than what we believe as Christians. I would agree, *if* we must make a choice between either believing *or* doing. Yet surely what we do will follow from what we believe—provided we truly do believe it. In the end, I think Meyers and I would agree that the true test of our faith is how we live. To be a person of faith is to live a faith-filled, faithful life. And the marks of that life, following Jesus, are to love God with heart, mind, soul, and strength, and to love our neighbors as ourselves. A faithful allegiance to this conviction is absolutely core to a truly progressive Christian faith.

---

3. Gorman, *Becoming the Gospel*, chapter 3.

CHAPTER 5

Searching for Jesus

IN OUR PITTSBURGH CHURCH newsletter we announced a Bible study course for women entitled *Who Is This Jesus? A Bible Study for Women*. In the process, however, we very nearly perpetrated one of the most disastrous church publication bloopers of all time. Fortunately, a critical error was caught in the first draft that was circulated among the church staff for proofreading. The first line was right: "*Who Is This Jesus?*" But the second line was astonishing. It was supposed to read, "*A Bible Study for Women.*" However, the "y" had been omitted from the word "*Study*." Plenty of strange things have been claimed about and for Jesus over the centuries, but that one would surely have been a first. Thank God for careful proofreading!

But seriously, who was Jesus, really, essentially? How did he understand himself, his role, his mission? Yes, surely, faith matters immensely. But facts matter too, particularly in an historically grounded faith such as Christianity. If facts matter, then the findings of archeological research and literary/historical criticism matter. So we must ask, what did Jesus *actually* teach? What did he stand for? What did he do . . . and die for? But the answers may not be as easy or simple to come by as we might wish. Most readers will probably be aware that there is a good deal of doubt, debate, and disagreement among New Testament scholars concerning just what we can know with certainty about the historical Jesus.

Many contemporary New Testament scholars, especially those associated with a group known as the Jesus Seminar, doubt that Jesus ever claimed to be the Messiah. Yet Bart Ehrman, one of the most skeptical of them all, argues in his *How Jesus Became God* that Jesus did make such a claim.[1]

---

1. Erhman, *How Jesus Became God*, 44–45.

Many decades ago, the renowned Albert Schweitzer authored a book enti-tled *The Quest of the Historical Jesus*. In addition to being a medical doctor, an accomplished organist, and a missionary to Africa, Schweitzer was also a professional Bible scholar. His book concluded that Jesus was a radical apocalyptic visionary who mistakenly expected the end of the world and the coming of God's kingdom during his lifetime. According to Schweitzer, when things didn't work out according to plan, Jesus precipitated his own death in a futile attempt to force God's end-time intervention.

Muslims, who revere Jesus as a virgin-born prophet and the one who will return to usher in the end of the world, believe that Jesus did not re-ally die on the cross but lived a full life and died a natural death. I have, in fact, seen with my own eyes the shrine in Kashmir that is reputed to be his tomb! Others in the West have variously portrayed Jesus over the years as a rugged religious entrepreneur, as a master salesman adept at winning friends and influencing people, as a Black Messiah, as a peasant Palestinian political revolutionary, or as a Zealot. Jaroslav Pelikan's book, *Jesus through the Centuries*, contains eighteen chapters, each with a different take on Je-sus throughout the past two thousand years, ranging from the Rabbi to the Cosmic Christ, from the Teacher of Common Sense to the Poet of the Spirit.

Dale Allison has set a challenge for us as we search for Jesus:

> There is more than one Jesus. There is the textual Jesus of antiquity, that is, the several canonical and extra-canonical presentations of him. There is the earthly Jesus of the first century, the man who spoke with Peter and Judas. There is the so-called historical Jesus, or rather the competing modern reconstructions of him. There is the Jesus of church history and tradition, or rather the numerous religious conceptions of him through the ages. And then there is Jesus as he is now, in his postmortem existence, the risen Christ, whom many claim still to encounter, in any number of ways. Jesus is not one but many.[2]

Since the very beginning of my ordained ministry in 1962, I have con-sistently found that most people want their minister to be honest with them, to talk straight about potentially controversial issues of Christian faith and life. From the start, for example, I made clear to prospective new members that our brand of Presbyterianism is officially non-fundamentalist. We are non-literalistic in our approach to the scriptures. We do not think, for

---

2. Allison, *Historical Christ*, chapter 2.

example, that it is necessary to choose between scientific accounts of the origin of the universe and the evolution of life on our planet on the one hand and a belief that God created all things on the other hand. Once we understand the non-literal nature of much biblical truth, we see that both can be true.

So who was Jesus, actually, essentially? Can't we just read the four Gospels and answer that question pretty easily? Well, not really. As we have just seen, in spite of all the information we have in the four Gospels, many different interpretations of Jesus have been drawn from the Gospel accounts. That is partly because the Gospels themselves offer us somewhat different stories with differing details and differing views of Jesus.

We must understand that the Gospels are not at all biographies in the modern sense of the term. That is to say, they aim to offer proclamations of faith rather than objective historical documentation. They were written by first-century believers to promote acceptance of Jesus of Nazareth as the Messiah, the Christ, the Son of God, the divine Savior. Decades elapsed between the original events and their eventual recording in the Gospels— probably forty years in the case of Mark, the earliest Gospel, and sixty to seventy years in the case of John, the latest.

While the first three Gospels differ from one another in important ways, the greatest differences are between these three and John. John is much more of an early theological document, placing in the mouth of Jesus long discourses and exalted claims for himself that are often in marked contrast to the Jesus we find in the other three Gospels. This is not to diminish John. It is, in many respects, my favorite Gospel. While John's witness does not aim for grounding in historical fact to the same extent as the other three, his truth about Jesus is more symbolic and metaphorical than factual—which is not to say that John's truth about Jesus is any less true than factual truth.

One of our church members in Pittsburgh used to say to me, repeatedly, "Give me the religion *of* Jesus, not the religion *about* Jesus." I do believe that distinction is important—the religion *of* Jesus/the religion *about* Jesus. While I don't think we have to choose between the two, I do believe churchgoers have often heard much more of the religion *about* Jesus. I strongly agree that we must honor the religion *of* Jesus. Surely, in order to be honest about our faith and honest to Jesus himself, we need to try to focus first on who Jesus saw himself to be, what he taught, and how he lived.

In spite of our acknowledgement that the Gospels are not historically objective accounts in the modern sense of the term, Christians do have grounds for a good deal of historical confidence in our faith. While the events and sayings of Jesus's ministry were recorded within a few decades of his death, the teachings of Buddha were not recorded until five hundred years after his death. The oldest existing manuscript of Homer's Greek epics dates to more than fifteen hundred years after Homer's time.

Theologian Hans Küng observed that "the New Testament manuscripts in our possession are much closer in time to the original writings, more numerous and in closer agreement with each other than any other ancient book."[3] The New Testament, notes Küng, is the most thoroughly investigated book in world literature. Over three hundred years of textual and literary analysis, historical research, and archeological investigations assure us of that.

What does all this come down to for you and me? I think the more we search for who Jesus really was, the more we will find ourselves standing where the earliest disciples stood. We will find ourselves asking with them, "Who is this Jesus? What does he mean to me . . . and for me? What kind of claim, if any, does his life make on mine? What will it mean if I decide to trust in him, to walk with him, to follow him?"

It is a good thing, I think, to walk where the earliest disciples walked, to walk with them even in their own questioning and uncertainty. We can no longer simply fall back on the authority of doctrine, helpful as it can be, as we wrestle with who this man Jesus really is for us. These questions about Jesus become very personal, very existential for us. Our answers become our own decisions about Jesus, a challenging, risky business of our own individual commitment.

In chapter 2 I told of the conservative young woman in our Pittsburgh congregation who challenged my progressive inclination to welcome with open arms those who had far more questions than answers about their faith. "What do we believe? What is our core?" she demanded. "Our core," I replied, "is centered on the first and essential question asked of those who join our Presbyterian Church: 'Is Jesus Christ your Lord and Savior?'" (There is more that follows upon this first question, as we shall see later on.) I went on to say to her that inevitably each of us must sort out for ourselves what it means to answer that question in the affirmative. We are all in the process, both individually and together as a Christian community, of sorting that

3. Küng, *On Being a Christian*, 147.

out. And when some folks cannot yet come to an honest affirmation of that core expression of Christian faith, they are still welcome to be a part of our community as we continue exploring and searching together.

Many Christians err on the side of emphasizing the divinity of Christ at the expense of the humanity of Jesus. The result can be a sad disconnect between his life and ours. We may then fail to see him as one who has known our own doubt, discouragement, and despair. We need to recall that the full humanity of Jesus stands on a firm foundation of biblical support.

Let's just roll some of the Gospel footage here to remind us of key moments in the life history of Jesus. At the outset we find him out in the desert, wrestling for forty days and nights with various temptations concerning his identity and destiny, about who he is to be and what he is to do. Is he to be one who succumbs to the temptation of achieving worldly power through miraculous displays and astonishing divine feats? If he were not fully human, then why would such questions arise at all for him?

Later we hear him readily confessing his own ignorance of certain matters—when he is asked, for example, about God's timing for the end of the world (Mark 13:32; Matt 24:36). To one who addresses him as "good rabbi," he responds, "Why do you call me good? No one is good but God alone" (Mark 10:18; Lk 18:19). On another occasion we see the very human Jesus shedding tears over the death of a friend (John 11:36). Astonishingly, we even see him allow a gentile woman to gently but firmly correct his own vision about whether or not his mission of mercy extended beyond the Jews (Mark 7:24–30; Matt 15:21–28).

In the heat of bitter conflict with the scribes and Pharisees we hear Jesus utter some very human, very harsh words that might even leave us to wonder if, on second thought, he would have chosen different terms for addressing those admittedly difficult, challenging folks. After all, he did teach that we should love our enemies and pray for those who persecute us. Yet on the first day of the last week of his life, we see him in a fit of anger overturning the tables of moneychangers in the temple, thus sealing his fate with his opponents.

At the end, on the night of his crucifixion, we find a thoroughly human Jesus in the Garden of Gethsemane, agonizing with God over his impending death, pleading that his life might be spared (Matt 26:36–39). Finally, on the cross we hear him as he cries out from the depths of a very human doubt and despair, "My God, my God, why have you forsaken me?" (Mark 15:34; Matt 27:46)

Even if each and every one of these scenes is not viewed as having actually occurred, they certainly add up to big-picture Gospel accounts of Jesus as leading a thoroughly human existence. Unless we understand the full humanity of Jesus, we are very likely to misunderstand him, what he stands for and what he asks us to stand for. Many Christians who put their total emphasis on his divinity tend to neglect his role as Jewish rabbi and prophet. "Jesus," they say, "is far more than a teacher and prophet. He is our divine Lord and Savior who died on the cross to save us." But if we emphasize only his miraculous birth, his miracles, his death and resurrection, all the while neglecting how he lived and the content of his teachings, I'm afraid that we have not truly understood him. We have not honored his own sense of his divine mission and purpose. We have not comprehended the earthly vision and way of life to which he calls those who would follow him. I believe it is at this very point that progressive Christianity, in an honest search for the historical Jesus, stands on solid biblical footing.

Let's get more specific. In the teachings of Jesus—at least in the first three Gospels—we find that Jesus's emphasis is not so much on himself as on the kingdom of God, the reign of God. We find that the teachings of Jesus are deeply rooted in the Hebrew tradition. When we consider what God asks of us, Jesus answers straight out of the law and the prophets—to love God with all our being and our neighbors as ourselves. Jesus can and must be understood as one of the Hebrew prophets, calling the people of God back to the basics of their faith, to sort out the essentials from the nonessentials, to get to the heart of it all, to see the big picture.

Furthermore, it emerges loud and clear that Jesus's vision of the domain in which God reigns is a humane vision of a realm of mercy and compassion, justice and peace and fairness for all. It is a humanitarian vision of God's good will for everyone, especially for those left out and left behind. Jesus envisions a realm where life's inequities and injustices are redressed, where the last shall be first and the first shall be last, where women and children and foreigners and sinners and the poor and the sick and infirm count just as much with God as anyone else.

With this humane, humanitarian vision in view, Jesus answered those legalists who objected that by healing the sick on the Sabbath he was violating the day of rest: "The sabbath was made for humankind, and not humankind for the sabbath" (Mark 2:27). This is why he tangled so much with these folks, because they seemed to care so much more for the fine points of the law than they did for people in need. So Jesus said to them,

41

> Woe to you, scribes and Pharisees, hypocrites! For you tithe mint,
> dill, and cumin, and have neglected the weightier matters of the
> law: justice and mercy and faith. It is these you ought to have prac-
> ticed without neglecting the others. You blind guides! You strain
> out a gnat but swallow a camel! (Matt 23:23–24)

This is a warning not only to Jesus's fellow religionists of his own time, but also to Christians of all times. It is a warning that, if we profess Jesus as divine Lord and Savior, we must not neglect the humanitarian concerns that are so clearly central in his teachings. Yes, we ask those who are making their first and/or renewed profession of faith in a Presbyterian church: "Is Jesus Christ your Lord and Savior?" There is, however, an additional question: "Do you trust in him? Do you intend to be his faithful disciple, obeying his word and showing his love to your life's end?"

According to Matthew, in Jesus's parable of the sheep and goats he made the challenge abundantly clear to all regarding what it means to follow him. Here's the scene: All nations, all souls stand before God to face their final judgment, their eternal destiny. What is the deciding question? Where does Jesus himself draw the line with an "or else" warning? As radical as it might sound to some ears, it will rest not on who has professed to know and believe in Jesus. It will come down to the question of who among us has treated our fellow human beings in need with mercy, feeding hungry ones, clothing the naked, welcoming strangers, visiting those sick and imprisoned (Matt 25).

"Where will you spend eternity? Heaven . . . or Hell?" In my childhood, on family road trips eastward on route 66 through Oklahoma and Missouri, I often saw billboards displaying this threatening query. It carried the implied warning: "Confess Jesus Christ as your Lord and Savior . . . or Else!" Yet in reality, that message simply doesn't square with Jesus's message about God's standards for our last judgment.

I know there are some Christians who have trouble fitting this picture into a strict theology of salvation by grace alone through faith alone in Christ alone. For them it simply sounds too much like salvation by good works. But, my friends, it's in the book. Jesus could not have made this point any clearer when, on another occasion, he is heard to say: "Not everyone who says to me, 'Lord, Lord,' will enter the kingdom of heaven, but only the one who does the will of my Father in heaven" (Matt 7:21).

No one has been any more insistent on this point than Jim Wallis, evangelical social justice activist. Conservative evangelical Christianity, he says, too often cuts the nerve between Jesus's kingdom teachings and his death on the cross. So it produces another sad disconnect—this one between, on the one hand, what Wallis calls the "atonement-only gospel," focused exclusively on how Jesus gets us delivered from hell to heaven, and on the other hand, "the kingdom gospel," with its call to live into God's kingdom here and now. In this view, says Wallis, Jesus "might as well have just gone straight to the cross to make atonement for our sins. In that case, why worry about this world? Why not just focus on heaven?"[4]

What I have dubbed as searching for "the big-picture Jesus" surely gives us overwhelming Gospel evidence that Jesus taught a thoroughly humane and humanitarian vision of God's will for humanity—of what it means to pray, "Thy kingdom come, thy will be done on earth as it is in heaven." Did Jesus actually read Isaiah 61:1–3, as in Luke's account of his keynote message at his hometown synagogue in Nazareth, declaring those verses to be fulfilled in himself? What can be said with certainty is that his ministry itself demonstrated his reported claim there:

> The Spirit of the Lord is upon me, because he has anointed me to bring good news to the poor. He has sent me to proclaim release to the captives and recovery of sight to the blind, to let the oppressed go free, to proclaim the acceptable year of the Lord (Luke 4:18).

Furthermore, there is solid evidence that Jesus thought of himself not only as herald of God's coming kingdom, but also as the principal embodiment of the kingdom's coming in and through his ministry. As Dale Allison puts it, "Jesus' starring role in the eschatological drama is all over the sources, in words attributed to him and in words assigned to others, in stories as well as in sayings."[5] Allison provides three pages of Gospel citations to substantiate this assertion. One leading example among the many is: "But if it is by the finger of God that I cast out the demons, then the kingdom of God has come to you" (Luke 11:20).

But did Jesus also think of himself as the Christ, the Messiah? If he did make or even imply such a claim—even while trying to keep it a secret among his close disciples—then rumors spreading of that claim would point to a primary reason for his crucifixion. Professing to be the Messiah might well mean claiming to be "King of the Jews," the charge that Pilate is said to have posted on his cross, a charge that the Romans would have

4. Wallis, *On God's Side*, chapter 3.

5. Allison, *Historical Christ*, chapter 4.

taken as a direct, seditious threat to their own rule. This is Bart Ehrman's line of reasoning about the cause behind Jesus's arrest and crucifixion.[6] Dale Allison agrees:

> [T]he safest and most sensible bet of all is that the Roman authorities executed Jesus as a royal claimant—"king of the Jews"—precisely because some people thought of him as such, and he did not repudiate them.[7]

It is has often been assumed that when Jesus identifies himself as the Son of Man, he is speaking of his humanity. Actually, the very opposite of that is the case. "Son of Man" is an even more exalted title than "Messiah," at least as that latter title was often used to refer to a promised earthly king and deliverer of Israel. This is the thesis of Daniel Boyarin, orthodox Jew and distinguished Talmudic scholar, in his 2012 book *The Jewish Gospels: The Story of the Jewish Christ*. The term "Son of Man," as used by Jesus in self-referral, would have represented a claim to fulfill Jewish expectations that go back to the book of Daniel. These were expectations that grew and developed throughout the two hundred years prior to Jesus. They were expectations that exceeded the traditional Jewish hopes for a new earthly descendant of King David, a Messiah to restore the earthly kingdom of Israel. Instead, these were hopes for a heavenly figure, a God-appointed ruler or viceroy, a divine-human, messianic Son of Man who would bring about God's reign on earth.

James Carroll, who in his insightful book *Christ Actually* draws heavily upon Boyarin's work, states the case clearly:

> Against the overwhelming weight of much historical Jesus scholarship, it was not that "Hellenized" followers of Jesus, coming long after him, invented a new idea of divinity—"Christ"—and shoehorned the Galilean peasant into it, but that, as "Jesus," his story naturally fell into . . . a profoundly Jewish narrative, as "Christ," that had been there long before he came along.
>
> Recognizing this should mark the end of the debates between those who see "Jesus" as human (and Jewish) and those who see "Christ" as divine (and universal). The understanding of Jesus as a somehow divine Messiah figure, the man-God already firmly rooted in Jewish thought, almost certainly marked those who responded to him at the start. Jesus himself, sharing their worldview

---

6. Erhman, *How Jesus Became God*, 44–45.

7. Allison, *Historical Christ*, chapter 4.

as a Jew of his time, could quite readily have understood himself in these terms as well. The End time is here. And so is the Son of Man.[8]

Now, beyond this, did Jesus possibly foresee and forecast his own death? Did he see it as part of God's plan, his own divine mission? Did he see himself as divine Redeemer of the world, sent by God to deliver humanity from sin and evil? We will return to these questions in chapter 11, but next we explore further what Jesus had in view when he preached the kingdom of God and called his followers to enter it.

8. Carroll, *Christ Actually,* chapter 3.

CHAPTER 6

God's Kingdom of Justice and Shalom

MARK REPORTS THAT JESUS began his ministry with this keynote: "The time is fulfilled, and the kingdom of God has come near; repent, and believe in the good news" (Mark 1:15).

The kingdom of God: the English phrase does not do full justice to the term as it is expressed in either Hebrew or Greek. In both languages a more dynamic, active sense is communicated. "The reign of God" or "the rule of God" might be a better translation. Without doubt, this reign of God was the unmistakable focus of concern for Jesus throughout his life and teaching and ministry.

It is quite possible that there were those who thought that Jesus's proclamation of the kingdom involved advocating a political revolt against Rome. Mainline New Testament scholarship, however, does not support Reza Aslan's proposition that Jesus was a Zealot, as advanced in his popular book, *Zealot: The Life and Times of Jesus of Nazareth*.[1] There is simply too little biblical evidence for that, plus far too much emphasis throughout his teachings on peace, love, and non-violence, to make at all plausible the notion that Jesus was a violent revolutionary.

On the other hand, the reign of God proclaimed by Jesus was not a purely spiritual, other-worldly realm. Jesus was not a Zealot, but neither was he an Essene. The Essenes—a Jewish community, contemporary with Jesus, that produced the Dead Sea scrolls—rejected life in the world around them, withdrawing into monastic isolation. They deplored the rest of the world as

1. For a critical assessment see Nadler, Review of *Zealot*.

depraved, evil, corrupt, and irrelevant to God's reign. Focused on leading a holy life, they were preparing for the arrival of God's entirely other-worldly kingdom yet to come. Jesus, however, plunged into the midst of everyday life, proclaiming the relevance of God's reign with words drawn from the experiences of daily life along the seashore, in the home, the marketplace, the fields and vineyards, and in the courts and halls of government.

Yes, the reign of God announced by Jesus is surely a spiritual, transcendent reality. Yes, according to John he said, "My kingdom is not from this world" (John 18:36), but he also taught his disciples to pray for God's kingdom to come and God's will to be done *on earth* as it is in heaven (Matt 6:10; Luke 11:20). So his is an imminent kingdom, coming upon this world here and now, bringing a realm in which God's will is done here and now. Its coming is good news because it brings concrete, material good for humanity—peace, liberation, justice, healing, and wholeness—especially for the poor, the weak, the hungry, the sick and suffering, the oppressed, and the downtrodden. The blessings of God's reign are both material and spiritual.

Nowhere is the Jewishness of Jesus more apparent than in his vision of the reign of God and its centrality to his very being. The sovereign rule of God, King of the universe—it is a vision of life, of human existence, of ultimate reality that has its foundation in the first commandment, "I am the Lord your God . . . you shall have no other gods before me" (Ex 20:3). The sovereign rule of God, King of the universe—it is another expression of the *Shema*, the summary creed of ancient Israel, "Hear, O Israel: The Lord is our God, the Lord alone. You shall love the Lord your God with all your heart, and with all your soul, and with all your might" (Deut 6:4–5). Jesus, of course, cited the *Shema* as the first and most important of all the commandments (Mark 12:29–30).

Here it is valuable to recall Michael Gorman's words about the biblical understanding of faith as echoed in Paul's writings:

> In Paul's world the *pist-* word-family [root word in Greek for "faith"] usually indicates faithfulness, and it has been suggested by a number of scholars that although this word-family is difficult to render into English, especially with one word, a phrase like "believing allegiance," "faithful allegiance," or "trusting loyalty" comes close to conveying its core meaning in many instances.[2]

And:

2. Gorman, *Becoming the Gospel*, chapter 3.

> Paul seems to prefer the "faith" or *pist-* word-family to describe
> what the Old Testament refers to as love for God, which meant
> both a deeply felt affective relationship with YHWH and covenant
> loyalty to YHWH (i.e., fidelity, obedience).[3]

To embrace the reign of God in one's life means for Jesus that we cannot serve two masters. This is a radical monotheism. Neither money nor
possessions, not family or nation, no political or religious authority, not my
own status or success or righteousness—nothing in all creation can take the
place of the one true God as the one in whom we place our trust, our love
and loyalty. God and God alone is absolute.

This one supreme power of the universe is not, however, despotic or
tyrannical. This Divine Power is personal, even parental. Jesus taught his
disciples to address the Sovereign of the Universe as "Abba/Daddy," "our
Father" (Matt 6:9; Luke 11:2). He could also speak of God's love as maternal,
like a woman who searches for us as for a precious lost coin (Luke 15:8),
or as a mother hen who protectively gathers her brood of chicks under her
wings (Matt 23:37). Jesus calls men and women to respond to God not with
fearful subservience or groveling servitude, but with love—the same sort
of trusting affection with which daughters and sons embrace their mothers
and fathers. And Jesus's vision of the reign of God includes our loving one
another as sisters and brothers, children of the same sovereign parent. This,
he said, is the second great commandment: As we are first and foremost
to love God with all our being, so then we are also to love our neighbor as
ourselves (Mark 12:31). These two are inseparably linked; it must be both/
and, God and neighbor.

There is another radical element in Jesus's teaching at this point. Living within the reign of this loving God, Jesus calls us to love as radically as
God loves. To believe in, to trust, that Divine Love is the Supreme Power
of the universe means adopting God's perspective on all persons, on all
creation. We are to love universally as God loves universally, to love as Jesus
loved—the wayward and the outcast, to love even our enemies and those
who persecute us and sin against us (Matt 5:44; Luke 6:35, 7:27, 17:4).

When Jesus calls us into the kingdom, he calls us to a radical allegiance to God's cause and to God's cause alone. At the same time, God's
cause on earth is the welfare, the well-being of all humanity. We could call
this "humanistic monotheism." This is not to say that Jesus was a modern secular humanist. He did not make humans the measure of all things.

---

3. Ibid., chapter 3.

But he did worship and serve, and call others to worship and serve, a God whose chief purpose in human history is the good of humanity, the health and wholeness, the liberation and restoration of all people, especially the least and the last, the lonely and the lost. God's will for all is *shalom*, which really is best translated as "comprehensive well-being."

While there are notable exceptions on both sides of the evangelical/ progressive Christian divide, the gulf between the two has probably never been greater than when it comes to understanding the personal versus the social significance of Jesus's mission and ministry. According to most evangelicals, Jesus came to save individuals from personal, individual sins through his saving death on the cross. According to progressives, he came to announce and initiate the upside-down-turning action of God's kingdom, instituting justice and fairness for all, especially those oppressed and exploited.

In support of their case, progressives have, of course, Jesus's own announcement of his purpose in the "keynote" message he delivers, according to Luke, at his hometown synagogue in Nazareth when he reads a passage from Isaiah, implicitly claiming it to be fulfilled in himself:

> The Spirit of the Lord is upon me,
> because he has anointed me to bring good news to the poor.
> He has sent me to proclaim release to the captives
> and recovery of sight to the blind,
> to let the oppressed go free . . . (Luke 4:18)

We need to keep in mind that the word "anointed" is the word from which the Hebrew word "Messiah" is derived. Thus Jesus the Messiah in Hebrew = Jesus the Christ in Greek = Jesus the Anointed One in English. The term was used in reference to the kings of Israel who were seen as anointed by God to their roles. So Jesus, by quoting the passage above, is describing his work as that of the divinely chosen sovereign who comes as liberator, as deliverer, and as savior of poor, oppressed, enslaved peoples.

All this fits perfectly with Hebrew notions of the righteous/just king, notions of what the good king is to do. Psalms 72 and 146 clearly show us this understanding. The good king uses his power to redress unfair imbalances in society, to rescue and defend and uphold the cause of the poor, to put down the rich and powerful oppressors. Luke also draws upon this tradition when he reports that Mary, mother-to-be of the Messiah, sang out in anticipation of God's work through the son she was to bear:

> God has brought down the powerful from their thrones,
>> and lifted up the lowly;
> he has filled the hungry with good things,
>> and sent the rich empty away (Luke 1:52–53).

Jesus is the one sent by God to usher in the reign of God, to overturn unfair and oppressive powers, and to establish a realm of mercy and justice for all. Whether Christians of all stripes realize it or not—and very often they do not—this is the socially and politically radical tradition out of which our language has emerged when we profess Jesus as Messiah, as Christ, as Lord and King. And this radical tradition goes all the way back to the liberator Moses, through whom God led a revolt of slaves out of bondage into liberty.

Jim Wallis has said it so well that a somewhat lengthy quotation is warranted:

> "[J]ustice" and "righteousness" are deeply connected in the Bible. They are richly applied to many things, from fair weights and measures, to just legal proceedings, to good personal conduct, to honesty and truthfulness, to an individual's right or just claim, to employers' economically just behaviors, to judges' fair decisions, to the governmental responsibilities of kings and rulers. The clear meaning of "justice" is "what is right," "rightness," or "what is just" or "what is normal," the way things are supposed to be. Fair and equal treatment under the law and the fairness of laws are common biblical concerns. Throughout the Scriptures, God is the defender and protector of the poor, the alien, the debtor, the widow, and the orphan. Justice can also mean "deliverance" or "victory" or "vindication" or "prosperity"—but for all, and not just a few. Justice is part of God's purpose in redemption. One of the clearest and most holistic words for justice is the Hebrew *shalom*, which means both "justice" and "peace." *Shalom* includes "wholeness," or everything that makes for people's well-being and security and, in particular, the restoration of relationships that have been broken. *Shalom*, the Bible's best word for justice and peace, is about restoring relationships. Justice, therefore, is about repairing the relationships that have been broken: our relationships both with other people and to structures and systems, systems of courts and punishments, money and economics, land and resources, and kings and rulers.[4]

There was once a time when evangelical Christians realized, claimed, and acted upon such convictions as their biblical heritage and mandate.

---

4. Wallis, *On God's Side*, chapter 12.

Evangelical Christians like William Wilberforce fought for the abolition of Britain's slave trade. Evangelical Christians in the United States fought for the abolition of slavery, for workers' rights, and for prohibition. Following the defeat of prohibition, evangelicals fell largely silent in the public square. But in recent decades they have reasserted themselves and increasingly displaced mainline, progressive religious voices. Evangelicals like Pat Robertson, the senior and junior Jerry Falwells, Franklin Graham, and James Dobson of Focus on the Family have rallied politically active followings in support of an agenda that generally stands opposed to greater rights and opportunities for marginalized people, opposition to government in general (except for the military and the restriction of LGBT and abortion rights), and advocacy for unfettered free enterprise—all taken up with a vengeance as their "godly" causes. All these evangelical leaders have been outspoken supporters of Donald Trump.

For many Christians, both left and right, there is often an either/or dichotomy between Jesus as the Savior, who delivers individuals from sin and damnation, and Jesus the good, liberating King, who delivers human society from systemic injustice and oppression. But there is a vital and necessary link between these two perspectives regarding the divine mission of the Christ. Both as liberating Messiah and as suffering servant, his work is to save, to deliver, to redeem, to liberate, to restore, to put things right, and to make things whole. These two poles of Jesus's redemptive mission must be kept in balance to order to affirm the holistic, comprehensive nature of the deliverance he brings the world.

Jesus comes as God's appointed, anointed regent to usher in God's kingdom, to deliver us all—especially those most in need of it—from injustice and oppression of all kinds, certainly in the political, social, and economic realms. But he also comes as healer and redeemer, to bring deliverance from the personal and individual oppressions that deprive us of true and abundant life—illnesses and diseases of mind and body, burdens of sin and guilt, expressed in addictions and dysfunctions and sicknesses of the soul. Surely it would take the work of the most just and merciful, the most fair and kind rulers the world has ever known, plus the ministries of Moses and the prophets, of Albert Schweitzer, Sojourner Truth, Mother Theresa, and Martin Luther King, Jr., plus the most effective evangelical preachers of the ages all rolled into one, to begin even remotely to suggest the comprehensive wholeness, the *shalom* that Jesus offers us as Messiah and Healer, as Suffering Servant, as Lord and Savior of all.

There will be more to say in coming chapters about living into the kingdom, about the way of Jesus, about discipleship. In conclusion here, however, let us consider one more implication of Jesus's view of the sovereign reign of God that profoundly shaped who he was and what he did. It was the source of his prophetic courage, his willingness to challenge the powers that be—whether the religious establishment or the political power structure, whether standards of sacrosanct tradition or popular expectations of his contemporary culture. Jesus was his own person in the face of them all. Before the pretentions of the Jewish high priest or the Roman governor, Jesus showed no awe or deference or fear.

So it was Jesus's closeness to God and to God's reign that placed in perspective for him every other claim upon human lives. Every earthly power, every possible claim to our trust, allegiance, and devotion that might captivate, enthrall, or oppress us—all this for Jesus was unmistakably finite and relative, and possibly idolatrous. Because he lived so thoroughly within the realm of God which he proclaimed, Jesus lived and died a free man. The risk entailed in such courage and freedom foreshadowed his cross, leading him eventually to his death. But he could walk that path with the ultimate trust and confidence in God that Martin Luther expressed in his powerful, immortal hymn: "The body they may kill; God's truth abideth still. God's kingdom is forever."

CHAPTER 7

Knowing, Loving, and Praying to the God of Jesus

ONCE MORE, MICHAEL GORMAN'S discussion of the meaning of the Greek root word for faith deserves our attention:

> Paul seems to prefer the "faith" or *pist-* word-family to describe what the Old Testament refers to as love for God, which meant both a deeply felt affective relationship with YHWH and covenant loyalty to YHWH (i.e., fidelity, obedience).[1]

Surely the allegiance to God's reign that Jesus affirmed was more than devotion to an abstract principle. It was a rooted in "a deeply felt affective relationship . . . and covenant loyalty," arising from a personal relationship with a personal God whom Jesus taught his disciples to approach in prayer as "our Father," "Abba," "Daddy." No doubt Jesus himself was nurtured in such a relationship: the Lord who is our shepherd (Psalm 23); the God of the prophet Hosea, who loves his people Israel like a faithful spouse who loves and forgives an unfaithful marriage partner.

I believe this relational foundation is the source of our Christian profession that Jesus is divine, God, Lord and Savior. We make that profession because we experience in Jesus a loving claim upon our lives, our affections, and our allegiances, a claim that can be none other than the claim of God. Meeting Jesus the Christ is, indeed, what this is about, responding to Jesus's dual invitations to "Come and see" and "Follow me" (John 1:39, 43). Thus we are not making a claim of divinity for Jesus that might somehow be

---

1. Gorman, *Becoming the Gospel*, chapter 3.

substantiated by giving him, if we were somehow able, an Ancestry.com DNA test. It more closely resembles that claim made upon us by the love of another human being, our dearly beloved, our life partner, our soul mate. It is like the love that leads to the covenant of lifelong partnership in marriage, to the commitment that declares, "I love you in a way that claims and binds me to you in lifetime loyalty. I want to live with you faithfully in my heart and by my side forever." The difference is that, in the case of Jesus, that loving claim upon us is experienced as absolute, as divine. So day by day we pray to "see him more clearly, love him more dearly, and follow him more nearly."

Evangelicals often ask, "Have you accepted Jesus Christ as your personal Lord and Savior?" and, "Do you have a personal relationship with Jesus?" These questions, especially the second one, can make other Christians—moderate/mainline/progressive Protestants, Catholics, and Orthodox—cringe just a bit. Maybe for some the second question even has something of an "icky" feel to it, like some may get from that old evangelical hymn "In the Garden," where Jesus "walks with me and talks with me and tells me I am his own." Many non-evangelical Christians would likely much prefer the hymn, "Immortal, invisible, God only wise, in light inaccessible hid from our eyes."

It is true that if we understand God simply as Jesus, apart from a trinitarian context, we may easily come up short, left with a God who is too small, too personalized, without mystery, majesty, and transcendence. Progressives, furthermore, often go so far as to reject what Marcus Borg identifies as "supernatural theism." Put in its simplest terms, this is God as "the Man Upstairs," the old white-bearded Father-figure of the Sistine Chapel, knowing all, seeing all, controlling all. Surely, think progressives, this is an altogether too personalized, anthropomorphized God, created in humanity's own image. To quote Borg:

> Sometime in childhood, I began to think of the word "God" within the framework of "supernatural theism." Namely, "God" referred to as a supernatural being separate and distinct from the universe, a supreme being who had created the universe a long time ago. In addition to being the creator, God was also the supreme authority figure who had revealed how we should live and what we should believe.[2]

2. Borg, *Convictions*, 43–44.

Borg goes on to say that traditional parental imagery for God as Father fulfills a universal childhood desire for a cosmic parent who will continue taking care of us throughout life. This may also foster

> . . . an image of God as the authoritarian parent: the rule-giver and disciplinarian, the law-giver and enforcer . . . a "finger-shaking God" whom we disappoint again and again. And it is the God whose demands for obedience were satisfied by Jesus's death in our place.[3]

Borg recalls that the God of supernatural theism, who was a source of doubt and anxiety for him during his teens, became increasingly problematic for him during his agnostic college years, and then whom he finally rejected in his atheistic twenties. Eventually, however, Borg was able to reaffirm the reality of God by claiming a series of mystical experiences that led him to a "panentheistic" affirmation of God, a conviction that God is in everything and everything is in God. The mystical experiences Borg affirms are extraordinary occasions of an ineffable sense of a diffuse presence of radiant divine glory in and through everything, an overwhelming feeling of connectedness with all things, experiences carrying with them a conviction that this is what reality is truly like. At the same time Borg is quite clear that panentheism, unlike pantheism, is not simply an affirmation of divine immanence, a divine presence suffusing all things. Yes, panentheism affirms that God is *in* all things, yet God is also *more* than all things; God transcends all things. God is the mysterious "More," Ultimate Reality itself.[4]

If evangelicals often tend to reduce God to a highly personalized God of supernatural theism and of a Jesus who walks with us in the garden, thus making the mysterious, transcendent God too small and no more than intimately personal, don't progressives often lean toward the opposite fault—making God too remote and impersonal, an ill-defined diffuse presence, a faceless, impersonal, cosmic force?

So we might ask: How can Christians, believing that Jesus is the supreme revelation of what God is like, *not* believe that God is personal? How can Christians, taught by Jesus to pray to God as our Father, *not* believe that God is like a loving, caring parent? How can Christians, taught by Jesus to love and trust God with all their being, possibly love and trust an impersonal cosmic force? How can Christians who profess with John that "God is

3. Ibid., 44.
4. Ibid., chap. 3.

love" *not* believe—love being a supremely personal quality—that this God of love thereby must be personal?

Biblical arguments aside, one must also wonder how "God" with a capital "G" could refer to no more than a merely impersonal cosmic force. If such a force could give rise to our personal existence, could that force possibly be inherently anything less than we human creatures are—personal, self-conscious, possessed of memory, imagination, purpose, intelligence, and capable of love? If we say "God is love," aren't we thereby affirming that God is personal?

One of the biggest problems progressives often have with a personal God relates to affirming a God who hears and answers prayer. Felten and Procter-Murphy, in their book on Progressive Christianity, write:

> Truth be told, most people are "foxhole pray-ers," crying out in the midst of disaster: "Lord, if only you'd get me out of _____, I promise to do _____!" And if we're not making deals with God, we're treating the Divine like some sort of Santa Claus for adults: "I want, I want, I want . . ." Oftentimes, prayer is confused with magic—passionately stringing together the proper words into incantations in hope of conjuring up the power to realize our desires.[5]

Doubtless there is much to these objections, and to the problematic notions that God would capriciously answer some prayers for deliverance from illness, suffering, or disaster while rejecting others—or that failure to get the blessing I seek in prayer indicates that I am not sufficiently spiritual or righteous to deserve God's favor.

Still, one wonders if Felten and Procter-Murphy have never sometimes found themselves pushed to offer any foxhole prayers. I surely have. Our grandson Nicholas was born on January 20, 1999, twenty-four weeks premature and weighing just a pound and a half. It was touch-and-go for weeks, even months, as the doctors gave him a fifty/fifty chance of surviving, with even greater likelihood of being seriously disabled. He endured eye surgery, then heart surgery, and finally suffered E. coli pneumonia.

Prayers poured forth from all directions. Our congregation in Pittsburgh mounted a note board for our members to write down their prayers to send along with messages for Nicholas's parents in Houston. Our Muslim Arab family and friends (see Appendix C for more about this side of our family) offered up prayers in Damascus. Jewish friends saw to it that prayer

---

5. Felten and Procter-Murphy, *Living the Questions*, need chapter 18.

requests were stuck between the giant stones of Jerusalem's Wailing Wall. Jan and I took our prayers to Houston to uphold our son and daughter-in-law and to stand by the side of our tiny new grandson in neonatal intensive care. I took Nicholas in the palm of my hand—tubes and wires and all—baptizing him in the name of the Father and the Son and the Holy Spirit. All in all, his birth and his valiant battle to survive were spiritually profound experiences for us, both awesome and awful.

Finally on Mother's Day, just around the date that he should have been born, Nicholas left Texas Woman's Hospital for home. Today, thank God, he is handicap-free, strong, and healthy. Who can say for sure if all those prayers made the difference? But surely it is not out of the question to suppose that along with the other powers with which our Creator has endowed us—reason, intelligence, imagination, creativity, scientific/medical and technological inventiveness—that we have also been given spiritual gifts that, through intercessory prayer and/or meditative visualization, can make a difference.

Indeed, in spite of their many problems with popular, traditional understandings and practices of prayer, Felten and Procter-Murphy acknowledge:

> On the other hand, there's a whole new branch of neuroscience devoted to uncovering the connections between one's mind and body. Called "psychoneuroimmunology," it explores the effect that one's emotional and spiritual well-being have on the immune system. Double-blind studies have indicated that people who pray and are prayed for recover more quickly than those not prayed for—a continued testimony to what we have yet to learn about our deep interrelatedness as a part of creation.[6]

The reference here to "our deep interrelatedness" is significant, since it would seem to imply that the power of personal connectedness is an essential component of prayer. Indeed, Felten and Procter-Murphy approvingly quote this passage from process theologian John B. Cobb about personal relationship with God through prayer:

> The function of prayer is to open ourselves to God's gracious working in our lives and to seek to align our own intentions with God's call to us. This should be the total stance of our lives, not limited to times of prayer. But surely prayer can be an occasion for focusing on this relationship and overcoming obstacles to it. As we

6. Ibid., chapter 18.

live more in harmony with God's purposes, we will act or pray as we are led, believing that what we do matters to others and to God as well as to ourselves.[7]

Marcus Borg as well, it should be noted, positively cites Martin Buber's notion of the "I-Thou" relational nature of the biblical God, affirming "moments in which we encounter 'what is' as a 'you' rather than as an 'it,' or an object."[8] He also asserts that being Christian "is about deepening relationship with God as known especially in Jesus,"[9] though he does not really develop that affirmation or associate it with his other eloquent, moving, accounts of mystical experiences that are not essentially personal in nature.

While I can enthusiastically endorse a universal mysticism and panentheism as Borg does, as well as the creation spirituality that Matthew Fox and John Philip Newell affirm, I also believe that this does not obviate Christ-centered mysticism and a belief that God, while being an immanent and transcendent creative cosmic force, is at the same time eminently personal. So: God is as personal as the personhood of Jesus; God is transcendent and mysterious; God is diffuse spiritual presence in and through all things. God is not just one or another; God is all of the above.

Perhaps Richard Rohr, author, spiritual guide, and retreat leader, has evangelicals particularly in mind when he objects to Christians saying simply that "Jesus is God," as if God were no more than what we see in Jesus. But the problem here is not about God being personal as Jesus is personal. The problem comes, Rohr says, when we try to understand Jesus "outside the dynamism of the Trinity" because "Jesus never knew himself or operated as an independent 'I' but only as a 'thou' in relationship to his Father and the Holy Spirit."[10]

God is love, affirms Rohr, and it is the dynamic of love's flow, uniting Jesus with God, drawing us and all creation into that dynamic union, so that where Jesus is (in God), we may be also (John 4:13). Simply put, for Rohr, this is what it means to believe in Jesus—that Jesus is, in his union with God, a stand-in for us all! This, says Rohr, is what Christian mysticism is all about, citing the Catholic Catechism that "Christian prayer is a communion of love with the Father, not only through Christ but also *in him*."[11]

---

7. Ibid., chapter 18.

8. Borg, *Convictions*, 40.

9. Ibid., 50.

10. Rohr, *Immortal Diamond*, 97.

11. *Catechism of the Catholic Church*, 2615.

CHAPTER 8

The Way of Jesus . . . The Way of the Cross

IF, AS MOST JESUS Seminar members apparently hold, the historical Jesus had no notion of his impending death as part of his mission, how is it that the very essence of his teachings, the path of discipleship onto which he calls us, points toward a path of self-sacrifice? The way of Jesus, even when his teachings make no explicit reference to the cross, centers on self-denial. Did he actually tell his followers to take up their own cross, to be willing to suffer and die, to find their life by losing it? (Matt 10:38; 16:24; Mark 8:34; Luke 9:23) Even if the gospel writers read the memory of Jesus's death back into their accounts of his teachings, there are still these themes, again and again: Turn the other cheek (Matt 5:39; Luke 6:29); love your enemies and pray for those who mistreat you (Matt 5:44; Lk 6:27, 35); lend to anyone who would borrow (Matt 5:42); give not only the shirt off your back but your cloak as well (Matt 5:40; Luke 6:29); go the second mile (Matt 5:41); forgive others not just seven times, as was considered the rigorous standard, but seventy times seven (Matt 18:21–22). Humble yourself (Matt 18:4; 23:12; Luke 14:11; 18:14); give yourself in serving others (Mark 9:35; 10:44). Devote yourself to feeding the hungry, clothing the naked, welcoming the stranger, visiting those sick and imprisoned (Matt 25:35–36). When we take a big-picture look at the way of Jesus, it adds up to the way of a cross, of self-denial.

In Mark's summary of Jesus's message at the very beginning of his Gospel, Jesus comes proclaiming, "The time is fulfilled, and the kingdom of God has come near; repent, and believe in the good news" (Mark 1:15).

Repent. It was a key word often on the lips of both John the Baptist and Jesus of Nazareth. *Repent.* It literally means to turn around, to face and move in the opposite direction. It means to reexamine your life, your attitudes and values, your priorities and loyalties—whatever you have placed your trust in.

The new direction for your life is a *reset* determined by believing, by trusting in God's loving reign that brings healing and deliverance and dignity for all. To believe is not simply to accept a creed or a doctrine. It is to place your full devotion and trust in, to found your very life in, God and God's good purposes. Repentance is required because we humans have a pervasive proclivity for placing our trust somewhere else, in something or someone else, and not in God.

Repentance suggests such a radical reorientation that it amounts to a kind of spiritual death, dying to an old way of life. John the Baptist required baptism as a dramatic ritual expression of one's willingness to undergo the spiritual mortification of repentance. Perhaps Jesus submitted to baptism because, as on the cross, he was leading the way for us, embodying, as one of us and for us, the path of spiritual death and rebirth that John proclaimed. For Paul, too, baptism symbolizes the believer's joining Christ in his death and crucifixion, dying to an old self, arising to a new self (Rom 6:3–11).

All the teachings of Jesus about self-denial and self-sacrificial love are clearly echoed in the writings of Paul, who gives us, well before Mark's Gospel, the first century's earliest and most influential witness of Christian faith. Baptism as the rite of initiation into life in Christ, into the Christian faith and life, means letting the old self-centered self be drowned in order that a new God-centered and neighbor-centered self may be raised up out of the water.

Paul even declares that the Christian life following baptism is to be understood as a living sacrifice, offered up to God for a process of ongoing spiritual transformation. Following that declaration, Paul proceeds to outline the shape of this life offered in love to God and neighbor. It entails returning to no one evil for evil, blessing those who curse you, feeding your enemies if they are hungry, contributing to those in need, practicing hospitality to strangers, weeping with those who weep, associating with the lowly, being humble rather than arrogant, and even counting others as better than yourself (Rom 12).

To contemporary, secular ears all this has to seem terribly strange and unappealing, even repugnant. Any call to self-denial goes against the grain

60

of everything that our culture encourages us to believe about the importance of self-esteem, self-respect, self-reliance, self-assertion, self-promotion, and self-defense. Who on earth wants to be a Christian if following Christ means becoming a doormat for the world to walk over? Furthermore, if Jesus is teaching us to love our neighbors *as we love ourselves*, how can all this focus on self-denial be consistent with loving ourselves? Don't these teachings about self-denial take us right back to that same beaten-down point we know from the doctrine of original sin, back to teachings that can lead us to put ourselves down, that can cripple our sense of self-worth, that can weaken and disempower us?

Some years ago the Swiss Christian psychotherapist and theologian Paul Tournier addressed these questions in a number of his books. I came across *A Place for You: Psychology and Religion* at a time when I was struggling with depression, struggling to regain a grasp on self-worth and confidence. I found it helpful and insightful then, just as I have ever since. Tournier observes that some of those who sought his help were individuals who from childhood had been taught in their Christian homes that they were to put others first, to be self-denying and self-sacrificing. Sadly, says Tournier, they turned out to be wounded, crippled adults.

Today, in a self-indulgent secular culture like ours, with its blatant encouragement of narcissistic attitudes, it seems unlikely that Tournier would encounter many such individuals, even among devout Christians. So it's not just all-pervasive advertising relentlessly urging us to believe that we owe ourselves countless self-indulgences; it's also the prosperity gospel preachers filling megachurches with messages that we need only ask what God can do for us, not what we can do for God and for the neighbors God calls us to love. Thus, the teachings of Christ now go even more against the grain of popular notions about self-esteem and empowerment, highlighting an issue that must be of real concern to anyone who would take seriously the call to Christian discipleship.

Tournier's approach to this challenge was not to deny or minimize self-denial as central to the teachings of Jesus. But there is a previous word, he says, an original word from God that we must hear first, before we are truly able to hear the call to self-denial. In the beginning, God tells us that we are a good creation, made in the very image and likeness of God, that we are divinely endowed with marvelous gifts and powers, that we are charged to develop and employ those gifts and powers as co-creators, as stewards of all the rest of creation. This is God's first word to us.

So we must first hear and act upon God's first word. Only then are we truly able, in due time, to hear and act upon God's second word. God's second word, spoken to us in Christ, is a call to deny ourselves, to take up our cross, to be willing to sacrifice ourselves as we live out our discipleship through loving God with all our being and our neighbors as ourselves. But we cannot give up what we do not first possess. We must first know and believe that we are beloved of God, gifted and empowered by God. We must first claim ourselves, assert and fulfill ourselves, before we can hear and act upon the call to let go of ourselves.

Just consider the lives of Jesus and of Paul, these advocates of self-denial. These two are no doormats, no shrinking violets. These are big, bold lives. These are powerful personalities. These are God-inspired, God-empowered, daring and courageous characters. These are challengers of the status quo and speakers of truth to power. Leaders and risk-takers, they venture forth into their world, inspiring and empowering others, facing down danger and death.

For Jesus and Paul, then, dying to self must not mean what we might first take it to mean, especially if we are reading through the lens of Eastern philosophies. It does not mean extinguishing the self, annihilating the self, as if the self were the problem, as if the self must become a cipher. No, the ego is not an illusion to be repudiated, renounced, shed. Jesus rather speaks of losing your life *in order to find your life*. Paul talks of crucifying the old self *so that the new self may be raised up*. Both Jesus and Paul are pointing to our need to lose our false self in order to find our true self. We must relinquish the false self so that we can claim the true self. So, then, as Jesus implies in the second of his two great commandments, we are indeed enjoined to love ourselves, value ourselves, fulfill ourselves. . .*our truest and best selves*.

Richard Rohr has written extensively about the true self and the false self in his book *Immortal Diamond: The Search for Our True Selves*. The false self is, above all, attached—attached to various vanities, to material gain, to privilege and power and prestige. And, of course, the false self is inevitably anxious and insecure, anxious and insecure about the possibility of losing all these attachments.

Rohr is quite intentional, however, in clarifying that the false self is not necessarily all bad, and is, in fact, quite essential to our self-development. His approach is similar to Tournier's:

Actually your False Self is quite good and necessary as far as it goes. It just does not go far enough, and it often poses and thus substitutes for the real thing. That is its only problem, and that is why we call it "false." The False Self is bogus more than bad, and bogus only when it pretends to be more than it is. Various false selves (temporary costumes) are necessary to get us started, and they show their limitations when they stay around too long. If a person keeps growing, his or her various false selves usually die in exposure to greater light.[1]

Here, then, we are clearly facing one of the primary paradoxes, one of the principal *both/and*s of Christian faith and life. On the one hand, we are to believe and affirm that we are created in the image and likeness of God, that we are endowed by our Creator with marvelous gifts, powers, and potentials that we are called to develop and fulfill. On the other hand, as we pursue this calling, we must be aware that we can easily succumb to the temptation to become fully invested in the externalities of our own supposed self-creation. We can become that self-made man or woman who begins to worship his or her supposed creator—ourselves.

So in the midst of it all, as Christians, we find ourselves also called to let go of ourselves, to relinquish our attachments to the false satisfactions of ego, of pride and competitiveness, of recognition and privilege and power that so readily become the harmful side effects of our God-commissioned quest of self-fulfillment. All our attachments to these externalities of self-fulfillment can readily grow to separate us from God and neighbor. They become the false gods of an egocentric life that knows nothing of the relinquishment of self that true love requires. True love of the true self requires the reinvestment of self in the love of God and others. But, again, it is not the extinction of the self to which Christianity calls us. It is the *re-centering* of the self, the re-centering of ourselves in the love of God and neighbor.

A life of love is spiritually paradoxical. Love is a relinquishment of self, but it is also an attachment of self, *par excellence*. Our somewhat self-less love of spouse and children, of friends, community, and country are themselves attachments that may come between us and God, may, in fact, become idolatrous. As Rohr has noted, we can make our religion and our patriotism a cover for our fear and our hatred so that "The ultimate disguise by which you remain a mean-spirited person is to do it for God or country."[2]

1. Rohr, *Immortal Diamond*, 27.
2. Rohr, *Dancing*, 69.

Such idolatry may, in fact, be at its most intense and most dangerous when God-and-country are melded into one. This speaks to why the earliest Christians countered "Caesar is Lord" with "Jesus Christ is Lord."

Jesus spoke on several occasions of an attachment to God that must stand higher than our attachment to family (Matt 10:45, 12:50, 19:29; Mark 3:35, 10:29; Luke 14:26). In his parable of the Good Samaritan, Jesus made clear, as did the prophets before him, that our love of God and neighbor is to transcend boundaries of national, racial/ethnic, and religious identities. It is not to the defense of these identities and boundaries that we are called. It is not to a love of "my country, right or wrong" that we are called. It is to a loving response to neighbors in need that Jesus calls us, as demonstrated in his story of the non-Jewish Samaritan who went out of his way to care for a wounded stranger—an unknown, unidentifiable, but probably Jewish neighbor.

Living the Christian life is a walk along multiple razors' edges. There are razors' edges between ideals and realities, between non-violence and self-defense, between love of self and family on the one hand and love of distant neighbors on the other. Attachment to God, whom we are to love with all our being, produces both attachment and detachment in our daily living. *Absolute* attachment to God above all else, however, instills a sense of *relative* attachment to everything else that God calls us to care about—our own survival, self-development, and rightful self-interests, our families and friends and local communities, and nations. We live in tension between attachment to God and to the rest of these important, yet lesser, attachments. Sometimes, maybe even often for faithful disciples, these loves and loyalties will conflict.

During the Vietnam War and other wars and interventions that followed, for example, many American Christians found that their flag was leading them down one fork in the road while the cross was leading them down another, a path less taken. It was this very tension that led me in the early 1970s to focus my doctoral dissertation research, with Harvey Cox as my advisor, on the relationship between patriotic and religious loyalties. It was a topic that had been famously explored as "Civil Religion" by my first-year Harvard Divinity academic advisor, Robert Bellah.[3] My survey questionnaire found, by the way, the same positive correlation of factors associated with support for an "America First" agenda in 1973 as in the 2016

---

3. Bellah's initial foray into this topic was published as "Civil Religion in America." My unpublished dissertation is *Modernization, Nationalism and Religious Commitment.*

presidential election. Uncritical nationalist attitudes were more likely to be held by my respondents who were older, less educated, residing outside a metropolitan area, with lower income, less geographically mobile, and more theologically conservative.

We read the Sermon on the Mount and conclude that Jesus would lead us on an absolutistic, perfectionistic, uncompromising path. Yet there are other teachings that show a more nuanced, even pragmatic stance. What did Jesus mean when he taught his disciples to be as "wise as serpents and innocent as doves" (Matt 10:16)? Was he pointing to the need to strive for a balance between realism and idealism? At times, it seems, he even went so far as to recommend the "street smarts" of some unsavory characters, such as a dishonest bookkeeper who fudged the figures to save his own hide! (Luke 16:1–8) So, in trying to walk the path of idealism and realism, we rich American Christians must, for example, figure how we can faithfully balance our own books between what we spend on ourselves, our families, and our pets versus what we share with those at home and abroad in desperate need.

Still, when all is said and done, how can we really and truly expect to live the way of the cross to which Jesus called his disciples, to follow his demanding teachings to turn the other cheek, love our enemies, forgive without limit, and enter the kingdom as little children? Honestly . . . we can only try the best we can. We can try our best to approximate the way of Jesus, knowing that we are bound to fall short, knowing that in the end we must, as he said we must, become as little children spiritually, totally dependent upon God's grace rather than our own efforts. Maybe this is one reason he set the bar so very high. Telling us, as he did, that we are to be perfect as God is perfect (Matt 5:48) might be intended to show us just how much we must rely on God if we are even to start moving in that direction.

We encounter the same reality that increasingly challenged first-century believers. The kingdom has not yet come in all its fullness; we are still living toward it in a fallen world. Yes, we are called to live into it here and now, but we know all the while that we will never live fully within that kingdom until the consummation of all things, until the kingdom has come in all its fullness, and we and all things are perfected by God.

When one joins a Presbyterian church, this question is posed: "Will you be Christ's faithful disciple, obeying his Word and showing his love to your life's end?" And the answer is: "I will, *with God's help*." Perhaps it helps to think of this way of living as something we throw ourselves into each new day, *with God's help*, taking the plunge into discipleship, into and on to the way of the cross, just as we have begun our path of discipleship by taking the plunge into baptism.

CHAPTER 9

Who Needs a Savior?

HOLDING LITTLE VANESSA, OUR first grandchild, in my arms, I marveled anew at God's creative goodness . . . the wonder and the beauty of our intricate bodies . . . the wonder that we exist at all, that anything exists at all . . . the wonder of love that gives us birth, cares for us in our helplessness, and nurtures us to maturity. I took beautiful, beautiful Vanessa into my arms, into my heart, into my life as a blessed sacrament of God's grace and goodness.

From our home in Pittsburgh Jan and I had made the trip to meet Vanessa at her home in Los Angeles, where our son was finishing up his PhD at UCLA. During that visit, my son Andrew and I took a little camping trip to the Angeles National Forest, up in the San Gabriel Mountains, just a short distance from Los Angeles. For both of us it was a bit of a sentimental journey, reliving a wonderful camping trip in the Jemez Mountains of New Mexico that the two of us had taken together almost twenty years before, when Andrew was only ten or so. Now in the San Gabriels, just as we had in New Mexico, we pitched our tent at seven thousand feet, surrounded by stately pines, redwoods, and magnificent mountains. We hiked through the forest and into a mountain canyon along a spring-fed stream to a small waterfall and a pool of icy water so still and clear that I had to look twice to see it. In the evening we played Scrabble by firelight and shared an extra-large, extra-fine cigar to celebrate Vanessa's birth. That was a holy communion to me—with God, with nature, with my son who was also now a father himself.

Soon thereafter, back home in Pittsburgh, I stood in front of our manse in Point Breeze, transfixed by one of the most beautiful sunsets I had beheld in a long time. That immense golden orb seemed to hang forever on the horizon at the end of our street, casting a lovely hue of rosy orange on the treetops above my head. It was an eternal moment, a sacramental moment. It moved me to thanksgiving:

> For the beauty of the earth,
> For the glory of the skies,
> For the love that from our birth
> Over and around us lies.[1]

The Hebrew roots of our Christian faith are sunk deep in the soil of an earthy materialism. This may sound strange to those who are accustomed to making sharp distinctions between things spiritual and things material. For the Hebrew Scriptures, however, there is no such polarity. The material world is seen as the good creation of a good God whose presence is manifest to us in and through things physical. The spiritual blessings of God are often depicted in the Hebrew Scriptures in material terms—green pastures and still waters, an overflowing cup, a table spread with good things to eat. All the earth is potentially sacramental, a vehicle of God's grace and God's goodness. Material abundance is a gift from the hand of God the Creator, who has graciously arranged to satisfy the needs of all living things.

God created all things and called them good—including the human beings God made in the very image of God. This too is a clear message of the Old Testament. Our Creator has crowned us with God's own glory and made us just a little lower than the angels, just a little less than divine. We are co-creators with God and stewards on God's behalf of all creation. God has charged us to develop and utilize our God-given gifts and powers, to join God in the ongoing work of creation—planting and building, being fruitful and multiplying. Our natural bodies and appetites are expressions of God's good creation. The rightful satisfaction of our natural desires for food and drink and sexual union is potentially sacramental, cause for joy and thanksgiving to God.

Old Testament religion is neither world-denying nor self-negating. Our Hebrew roots serve to keep us Christians attuned to the goodness of God's material creation and to our own creation in God's image. Honoring these roots keeps us from succumbing to that sharp and invidious opposition between things material and things spiritual, between the divine and the human, oppositions that have plagued certain expressions of

---

1. *Glory to God* 14.

Christianity through the ages up to the present day. I think, for example, of the misguided asceticism and self-flagellation in certain expressions of medieval monasticism. I think of certain forms of Protestantism, with their world-denouncing attitudes, their teachings of total human depravity, their renunciation of the world as the domain of the devil to be consigned to hellfire and eternal damnation, their withdrawal from social responsibility, and their refusal to do anything to make this a better world here and now because Christ is coming again soon, the expression of a morbid fixation on the coming Armageddon when a wrathful, vengeful God will destroy the vast majority of us and save only them, the righteous few.

How much damage to human self-esteem has been perpetuated by the traditional Christian teaching of original sin? Haven't countless multitudes of boys and girls, men and women been put down, kept in place, miserably subjugated through the centuries by the horrible notion that they are worthless, degraded creatures who deserve nothing more than God's everlasting wrath? Hasn't this distorted view of human nature, in fact, been used by the church, by priests and preachers, by those in various realms of authority to convince us that our souls are in mortal jeopardy without what the church and other God-ordained authorities alone can offer—that we are lost and damned without confession, absolution, repentance, conversion, or being born again—unless our lives are directed and controlled so that we are kept on the straight and narrow path toward eternal salvation?

Progressive theologians like Matthew Fox and many others in recent years have offered a much-needed corrective to this one-sided negative view of human nature. John Philip Newell, for example, of the same "creation spirituality" school as Fox, has sought to rehabilitate the teaching of Pelagius, an early Celtic theologian who took a far more positive view of human nature than Augustine. Pelagius lost the debate to Augustine, however, and was ever thereafter branded within Roman/Western Christianity as a heretic to the orthodox tradition.

Still, even though we have been moving in more positive directions, to this day one of American Christians' most popular hymns, "Amazing Grace," has us declaring ourselves to be "wretches." Liturgies still in use in some Anglican churches continue to have worshippers confessing that "there is no health in us." Not a few Calvinists (a good many Southern Baptists among them) still teach the "total depravity" of humanity, perhaps in ways that distort the original meaning of what is, nevertheless, a most unfortunate term. Surely such views can only cripple psyches, undermine self-confidence, stifle creativity, and constrict human potential, prospects, and horizons.

So why not abandon the whole notion of original sin altogether? Suppose we just affirm that human beings, however wayward at times, have been from the beginning—and remain ever since—beloved offspring of their Creator. Suppose further that we also challenge the whole notion that Christ died on the cross to save us from sin (more about this in Chapter 11)—a view that seems increasingly to prevail within progressive Christian circles. But where, then, does this lead the trajectory of progressive Christian thinking today? Without sin, what need is there for salvation, for a savior?

Certainly there are awful wrongs to lament and from which to repent concerning much of traditional Christianity's teaching and preaching about original sin. But because it has so often been distorted, misconstrued, applied in cruel and abusive ways, ought we to abandon the notion altogether? Might we not then be forfeiting an essential key to understanding the complexities of human nature, of human history, politics, society, and economics—indeed, the complexities of our own individual psyches?

For decades now, our popular culture has been obsessed with evil, with serial killers, with the very darkest sides of human existence. Our daily news cycles are filled with unspeakable horrors, atrocities, genocides continuing well into the twenty-first century, defying the twentieth century's post-holocaust cries of "never again." Isn't it at best ironic, therefore, that during these same recent decades many progressive Christians have been putting increasing distance between themselves and the notion of original sin?

In his *Convictions,* Marcus Borg devotes precious little attention to the subject, though in his treatment of the Genesis story of Adam and Eve's "paradise lost" he does refer to the universal fault of "making oneself the center of one's concern and thus the center of existence."[2] Felten and Procter-Murphy acknowledge the reality of evil and concede that "The power of the demonic is the power of us—the power to reject God and to thwart the emergence of life, love, and what is possible."[3] But they do not really develop this line of thinking, nor give any consideration to how we might be delivered or redeemed from evil. What they offer instead is the promise of a spirituality of creativity and transformation that seems

2. Borg, *Convictions,* 121.

3. Felten and Procter-Murphy, chapter 10.

unrelated to Christ's death and resurrection, except as a model or example of how each of us might hope to experience spiritual renewal. Nowhere in their writing do we find Christ as the *agent* of our deliverance from sin and evil. Furthermore, they assert:

> The communities associated with the Gospel of Thomas and "Q" (from which Matthew and Luke get many of their stories) don't even have crucifixion and resurrection stories. The doctrinal savior language was really only brought to flower in the fourth-century creeds.[4] [Wouldn't Paul be surprised?!]

Liberal Christian theology in the late nineteenth and early twentieth centuries both reflected and supported a general optimism about humanity's growing scientific and technological abilities to triumph over the old foes of ignorance and disease and incapacity. The mantra of French psychologist Emile Coue's "autosuggestion" approach to therapy, "Every day in every way, I'm getting better and better," was the watchword of an entire age. *Invictus* was its poem, with its final declaration, "I am the master of my fate: I am the captain of my soul." Man (not yet woman) the invincible! Humans, it was widely believed, were approaching the point where they could accomplish virtually anything to which they set their sights—including, for example, the construction of a gigantic and unsinkable ocean liner, a titan of the seas.

But the unsinkable became the unthinkable. And hard on the heels of the 1912 Titanic disaster's blow to human hubris and optimism there followed the far greater disillusionment wrought by the ghastly horrors of World War I—originally supposed to be, of course, the "war to end all wars." Out of these ashes arose, in just a few short years, the even more unimaginable evils of Nazism, driven by its fanatical, death-dealing drive to fashion a new superman within a super race. Simultaneously, in Russia, the Marxist/Leninist project was aiming for the construction, not only of a totally new society, but also of a totally new human. Seventeen million people died in the First World War; 50 million died in World War II, 80 million when deaths from war-related famine and disease are included. Estimates of how many of his own people Joseph Stalin killed range from 20 to 60 million.

During this same period, theological liberalism gave way to a new theological movement characterized as neo-orthodoxy. Karl Barth, Paul

---

4. Ibid., chapter 20.

Tillich, Reinhold Niebuhr, Emil Brunner, and others sought to reclaim classical Christian doctrines, such as original sin, reframed in non-literal ways. Niebuhr's thought was dubbed "Christian realism," due to his insistence on the centrality of a realistic assessment of our human propensity to self-interested, self-justifying behavior. According to Niebuhr, a critical yet constructive understanding of the social, political, and economic realms required nothing less than a complex, nuanced understanding of human nature. The teachings of the Bible, of Augustine and Calvin can lead Christians to maintain both high ideals and realistic insights. Human nature, Niebuhr affirmed, makes democracy both possible and necessary. Created in the image of God as co-creators with God, we are capable of self-governance. But as fallen creatures, we also need a democratic system of checks and balances to restrain our propensities to blind self-interest, abuse of power, corruption, and exploitation. Without a capacity for self-criticism or humility, Utopian thinking and systems—as so disastrously proven in the first half of the twentieth century—are doomed to failure.

In 1948 Scottish theologian Donald Baillie told the story of original sin as a symbolic metanarrative in his influential book *God Was in Christ: An Essay on Incarnation and Atonement*. In the beginning, says Baillie, it is as if God created human beings to be like children joining hands in a circle of dance, of loving and joyful play. God is at the center of that circle, uniting all in a harmony of love and delight. With the freedom God has also given us, however, the sad reality of our human condition is that we have dropped hands with one another. We have turned our backs on God and neighbor and struck out on our self-centered course, each one declaring, "I am number one. I will do it my way." It all begins with the good and loving Creator's intention for us, but then is broken by the faithless disobedience of Adam and Eve, our symbolic, primordial progenitors. Paradise has been lost, forsaken for the law of the jungle, dog-eat-dog and the devil take the hindmost.

Holy Scripture gives us the continuing story of human waywardness and divine faithfulness. God does not give up on God's creatures or on the beloved community. God is the "hound of heaven," relentlessly, redemptively pursuing us, finally coming embodied in Jesus to embrace us in love, to turn us around and bring us back into the circle, to restore us to lives that are once more centered in the love of God and neighbor. God has come to us in Christ, reconciling us to God, to one another, to our own true selves.

Augustine and Luther both saw sin as the heart turned or curved in upon itself. Paul spoke of an old self that needs to die. It is the self-centered self that needs to die, the self that is set against God and neighbor. Paul speaks, as well, of all creation groaning in bondage and travail (Rom 8:22), somehow alienated under the weight of our sin, a sad reality we now see ever more starkly as nature itself is brutally exploited for short-term self-interest. If sin, then, is essentially egocentricity, who on earth can possibly claim to be free of it . . . including the newborn infant? Is this not, in fact, the challenge faced by each and every human being—to grow up and out of the self-absorption of infancy and childhood, to consider the needs of others, to learn to share, to become a giver and not just a taker?

Feminist theologians have criticized traditional formulations of the doctrine of original sin—like Niebuhr's and Baillie's—because they focus only on prideful rebellion against God as the essence of it all, the notion that we all succumb to the serpent's temptation to become as gods ourselves. This may ring true, assert the feminists, for those circles of prominent, powerful men who have set doctrinal standards in the past. But what about women? Hasn't woman's failure, feminist theologians like Susan Nelson have asked, been more often to hide (just as Eve hid from God), to hide her gifts and abilities, her own unique identity, to stifle and deny herself?[5]

We can go even further, questioning what kind of sense the notion of sin as prideful rebellion can possibly make for those of any gender who are without much power, for those who are oppressed, abused, exploited, victimized. Has the doctrine not, in fact, been used as a tool of control, to suppress rebellion, to keep slaves obedient to masters, women subservient and submissive to overbearing and abusive husbands, and so on and on? Blaming Eve for Adam's sin even appears in the New Testament, with I Timothy 2:14 declaring, "Adam was not deceived, but the woman was deceived and became a transgressor."

While prideful rebellion against God can be a useful way to understand many expressions of sin, perhaps the notion of egocentricity or narcissistic self-absorption sheds a more comprehensive light. Infancy is total self-absorption. Abuse, victimization, trauma typically result in self-absorption. Of course, neither infancy nor victimization implies any taint whatsoever of moral fault or blame. We would surely not blame the infant or blame the victim for being an infant or a victim, so maybe we need words in addition to "sin": perhaps "alienation," or perhaps "alienating self-absorption." After

5. Nelson, *Healing*, 10–11.

all, if there is no deliverance, no liberation, no transcendence of infancy, or of prideful and arrogant egotism, or of victimhood, then the self-absorption of these various conditions is ultimately alienating. Self-absorption, whatever its form—expressed in clinging dependency and helplessness, or in domineering self-assertion, or in the nursing of wounds and wrongs and grievances—is alienating. This is surely not all there is to us, yet the alienation of egocentricity is inherent to the human condition.

While she doesn't use the word, pastor and theologian Fleming Rutledge essentially describes a state of alienation as she defines the condition of sin:

> To be in sin, biblically speaking, means something very much more consequential than wrongdoing. It means being catastrophically separated from the eternal love of God. . . . It means to be helplessly trapped inside one's worst self, miserably aware of the chasm between the way we are and the way God intends us to be. It means the continuation of the reign of greed, cruelty, and violence throughout the world.[6]

It has been observed that there is nothing like having children to convince one of the realities of original sin. While I surely could not look into the eyes of my baby granddaughter Vanessa and see there an original sinner, nevertheless, with memories of our son's and daughter's early years not so distant, I could understand that by the time Vanessa reached the terrible twos I might very well come to a different conclusion! Then too, of course, as our children become ever more challenging, we parents become ever more aware of our own shortcomings and limitations.

The Bible's comprehensive view on our human nature is neither unduly pessimistic nor unduly optimistic. It is what we might call "hopeful realism." It sees the two sides of the coin, the both/and of original blessing and original sin. The Bible does not give up on our human nature; it does not portray life in this world as a lost cause with no hope of redemption and improvement and reform here and now. But neither does it fall for easy Utopian schemes that promise through self-improvement, moral education, or political revolution the possibility of human self-salvation. From the perspective of the Bible's hopeful realism, we humans are not who we were intended to be. We do not readily grow beyond our egocentricity. We are often painfully captive to impulses to dominate and exploit the earth and one another, impulses that are, in the long run, self-destructive.

---

6. Rutledge, *Crucifixion*, 173.

Still, we are not inherently evil. We are originally blessed, created in the image of God. Although that image has been obscured and distorted, it has not been destroyed. We can be healed and restored by the redeeming love of God. The transforming love of God—together with the loving human agents God places in our lives—can begin to turn our hearts right side out, spinning us around, bringing us back into the circle of holy communion with God, with one another, with the natural world, and with our own best and highest selves. We can become again who we were meant to be—co-creators with God; agents of God's goodness and redeeming love; people who see and honor in one another the image of God; people who affirm the good world around them as a precious, divine gift to be received with gratitude, to be treated with all the respectful carefulness of a responsible stewardship, to be honored as the sacramental means of divine grace.

> God, brilliant Lord,
>> yours is a household name.
> Nursing infants gurgle choruses about you;
>> toddlers shout the songs
> That drown out enemy talk,
>> and silence atheist babble.
> I look up at your macro-skies, dark and enormous,
>> your handmade sky-jewelry,
> Moon and stars mounted in their settings.
>> Then I look at my micro-self and wonder,
> Why do you bother with us?
>> Why take a second look our way?
> Yet we've so narrowly missed being gods,
> bright with Eden's dawn light.
> You put us in charge of your handcrafted world,
>> repeated to us your Genesis-charge,
> Made us lords of sheep and cattle,
>> even animals out in the wild,
> Birds flying and fish swimming,
>> whales singing in the ocean deeps.
> God, brilliant Lord,
>> your name echoes around the world (Psalm 8, *The Message*).

This is God's good, loving intention for us humans and for all creation. God has created all things good, in love and for love. Love, said Jesus, is the be-all and end-all of our existence, to love God with all our being and our neighbors as ourselves. But absorbed in self, such love seems beyond us. Lost in self, we are lost indeed. We need salvation, healing (the root meaning of "salvation"), liberation, deliverance, redemption, atonement (at-one-ment with God and neighbor), reconciliation, and, yes, transformation. We need restoration to wholeness, to the true humanity that God has, from the beginning, intended for us. We need to be saved. We need a Savior.

CHAPTER 10

Jesus Christ, God's Restored Humanity

DID JESUS SEE HIMSELF as the Messiah? As the Son of Man? As the principal herald and agent of God's imminent kingdom? As fulfilling Isaiah's role of the suffering servant of the Lord who vicariously bears our sins? All of this is the very active subject of debate/disagreement to one degree or another among mainline New Testament scholars. Overall, however, not just adherents of the Jesus Seminar but "liberal" Protestant biblical scholars for many generations have doubted that Jesus himself made any claims of divinity for himself. Such claims must be the result of believing disciples having read back into the record their own professions of Christological faith, which in most cases reflected the influence of Greek rather than Jewish notions about any possible divine-human incarnation.

Astonishingly, however, from the Jewish side there now comes a very different reading to support the historicity of the Gospel claims. According to the highly regarded Talmudic scholar Daniel Boyarin (in his *Jewish Gospels: The Story of the Jewish Christ*), it is entirely plausible and completely in accord with Jewish traditions and expectations that Jesus did indeed claim that all of these roles were fulfilled in himself and in his ministry. These are not, according to Boyarin, later "Christian" claims fabricated in a Gentile world outside of and in contrast to Jewish convictions. No, consistent with his Jewish context, Jesus presents himself as the divine-human Messiah, the divine-human Son of Man come to earth as Redeemer, as Sovereign, as suffering servant of the Lord who fulfills that role as set forth in Isaiah 53! What would have been debatable among Jews of the time would not have been the plausibility and authenticity of these claims themselves, but whether or not Jesus was the one who fulfilled them. Some Jews, later to be known as "Christians," said "yes" while others said "no." In Boyarin's words:

> Jews at the same time of Jesus had been waiting for a Messiah who was both human and divine and who was the Son of Man, an idea they derived from the passage from Daniel 7. Almost the entire story of the Christ—with important variations to be sure—is found as well in the religious ideas of some Jews who didn't even know about Jesus. Jesus for his followers fulfilled the idea of the Christ; the Christ was not invented to explain Jesus' life and death. Versions of this narrative, the Son of Man story (the story that is later named Christology), were widespread among Jews before the advent of Jesus; Jesus entered into a role that existed prior to his birth, and this is why so many Jews were prepared to accept him as the Christ, as the Messiah, Son of Man.[1]

The notion of a Jesus as a single being in whom both the divine and the human are united is thus neither a late New Testament nor a post-New Testament invention. As we have previously noted in Chapter 5, a collective, representative figure, both human and divine, can be identified in the Hebrew origins of one called the Son of Man. Daniel 7:13–14 depicts the "Ancient of Days" (i.e., God) granting rule over the earth to "one like a Son of Man." This figure is said to stand for "the holy ones of the Most High" (7:18, 21–22) and for "the people of the holy ones of the Most High" (7:27), probably meaning the people of Israel as a whole. But this is also an individual figure, clearly *both* an earthly ruler/king *and* of divine origin. Boyarin points out that the Son of Man as a divine messiah is also clearly set forth in the apocryphal and deuterocanonical works of 1 Enoch and 4 Ezra. The Similitudes (1 Enoch 37–71) draw upon Daniel 7 in portraying a messianic Son of Man who is pre-existent and yet hidden, finally to be revealed as judge and ruler of all.

Many biblical scholars believe that a dual significance, both individual and communal, is also found in second Isaiah's Servant of the Lord figure, the anointed one of the Lord (messianic implications) whose identity Jesus claimed for himself in his inaugural message in Luke 4. In Isaiah's representation this Servant of the Lord appears to be both an individual and a collective representation of the whole people of Israel.

1. Boyarin, *Jewish Gospels*, chapter 2.

So also in Paul's New Adam (Rom 5:11–21)—Adam meaning "of the earth," and representing all humankind—there is the very clear affirmation of Christ as redemptive, the collective representation of, the embodiment of, and the restoration of our true humanity. As Adam bears within himself all humankind in his fatal, primordial fall from grace and alienation from God, so Christ bears within himself all humanity in one life fully offered to God in perfect unity with the divine will and purpose. The first Adam is all of us, for ill and for death; the second Adam is all of us, for good and for life. Christ comes to us as the embodiment of the restored human whom God intended Adam to be, the incarnation of the best and truest human. As one church member put it succinctly, "This New Adam is God's do-over!"

Christ as the New Adam in Paul's thinking is *both* the embodiment of God in Jesus as one human being *and* the embodiment of God in Jesus as all humanity. Furthermore, God in Christ *both* embodies the restored humanity that is God's intention for us *and* invites us into that reality through our incorporation into Christ's body, the church. In Christ God comes to us as one of us and as all of us, so that we, in turn, may be taken up into, incorporated into that new corporate human. The theme here is reciprocal, like a fugue, moving back and forth from God's incarnation in Jesus Christ to humanity's incorporation into Christ and thus into God—since Christ is in God and God is in Christ. So Paul testifies both to living in Christ and to Christ living in us.

A comparable notion of the corporate/representational nature of Christ is also found in the Gospel of John's imagery of vine and branches, also with fugue-like language. Christ is the vine and those who adhere to him are the branches, all one organism together. So John's Christ speaks of believers abiding in him and of himself abiding in believers. Furthermore, in John's account of Christ's lengthy prayer on the eve of his death (chapter 17), Jesus affirms that believers are one in him, just as he is one in God. Thus we have the astounding notion that as believers are one in Christ and Christ is one in God, believers are therefore one in God. With Christ we are taken up into the Godhead! To the extent that later formulations of God as Trinity may be found in rudimentary form in John's Gospel (and elsewhere in the New Testament as well), we can hear John's Christ declaring that in and through himself we are taken up into the life of the Trinity:

> As you, Father, are in me and I am in you, may they also be in us. . . .
> The glory that you have given me I have given them, so that they

may be one, as we are one. I in them and you in me, that they may become completely one (17:21, 22–23a).

This divine/human unity, this Christocentric mysticism, this deification of humanity is a theme, as we have seen, solidly grounded in the New Testament, with deep roots in Hebrew scripture as well. And all of this, of course, is perfectly consistent with the Genesis affirmation that humanity is created in the very image and likeness of God. For Christians this affirmation has its supreme fulfillment and manifestation in Jesus Christ, our divine/human, God/man, our own humanity restored to its original condition.

It cannot be emphasized strongly enough that these concepts are all corporate and communal. Our incorporation into God through Christ is in and through the church as the body of Christ. We are simultaneously united with God and with brothers and sisters in Christ. This is not individualized mysticism, not the total absorption of single souls into God. This is body mysticism: it is the restoration of a divine/human community. Yes, surely, the individual Christian can affirm with Paul that "Christ lives in me" and "I live in Christ." But this is never apart from our also being united with other believers as members together in the one body of Christ. John's vine/branches imagery conveys the same idea.

In the Eastern Orthodox tradition, this divine/human unity is known as *theosis* ("divinization"). St. Athanasius of Alexandria wrote, "He, indeed, assumed humanity that we might become God."[2] *Theosis* has long been a strong theme of Orthodoxy, often downplayed or even rejected in western Christianity. Still, as early as the second century, Bishop Irenaeus of Lyon, who brought eastern Christianity with him from Asia Minor, asserted: "Christ Jesus our Lord, the Son of God . . ." [became] ". . . the Son of Man that man in turn might become a son of God."[3] In recent years the *theosis* theme has been progressively rediscovered and reaffirmed in the West. Thus, in 1995, Pope John Paul II explicitly endorsed the *theosis* tradition, not just as central to Eastern Christianity, but also as claimed in the West as early as Irenaeus.[4] Then too, in recent decades there has been among Catholics and Protestants alike a discovery and reaffirmation of the Western mystics, including especially the sometimes-renegade women mystics such as Hildegard van Bingen, Teresa of Avila, and Julian of Norwich.

2. Athanasius, *On the Incarnation*, 93.

3. Irenaeus, *Against Heresies*, III. 10.2.

4. Pope John Paul II, "Orientale Lumen," I:6.

For Richard Rohr, divine/human union is the message of all religion, not just Christianity: "[D]ivine and thus universal union is still the core message and promise—the whole goal and the entire point of religion."[5] And, yet, Rohr also notes that it is precisely at this point that he encounters the greatest resistance and objection, especially from clergy, as if the notion of humanity's divinization were heretical, antithetical to the very essence of Christianity. Rohr counters by asserting that were he to list all the scriptural passages supporting *theosis*, it would entail virtually the entire New Testament. [Assuming, I would suppose, that one has eyes to see and ears to hear as Rohr does!] We have already referenced here some of those verses most central in Paul and in John, but here are a few more:

> . . . [God] has made known to us his will, according to his good pleasure that he set forth in Christ, as a plan for the fullness of time, to gather up all things in him . . . (Eph 1:9–10)
> And [God] has put all things under his feet and has made him the head over all things for the church, which is his body, the fullness of him who fills all in all (Eph 1:22–23).
> . . . so that you may be filled with all the fullness of God (Eph 3:19).
> Thus he has given us these things, his precious and very great promises, so that through them you may . . . become participants of the divine nature (2 Peter 1:4).

In addition, of course, there are the many scriptural references to humans as offspring and children of God. Do not children share the very flesh and bone, the DNA, of their parents? More conservative Christians will object, of course, that the New Testament also makes clear that after Adam's fall, with original sin in our bones, we can become God's children only by being adopted as such through Christ, repenting and being born again. This must remain an issue for our later consideration, but here we might ask what the parable of the prodigal son suggests on this matter. Was not the prodigal still his father's son even while he was yet in that far country of his waywardness? Did not his father rush out to welcome him home while he was still at distance, even before he had fallen to his knees in confession and repentance?

As for my own appreciation of the mystical tradition, I well remember hearing from my professors at Harvard Divinity School in the late 1950s and early 1960s that "mysticism begins in mist and ends in schism." Spiritual

---

5. Rohr, *Immortal Diamond*, 95.

disciplines and practices received scant attention in the classroom, while assiduous scholarship, rational analysis, and discourse were, of course, highly honored and rewarded.

After returning to Harvard to pursue doctoral studies later in that same decade, following a satisfying four years in parish ministry, I quickly began to feel the intense intellectualism and academic competition wearing thin and unsatisfying. Furthermore, something unfamiliar and foreboding started to creep up on me, something that I could not yet identify. At first it was a vague sadness and dissatisfaction, then a loss of zest and purpose, then anxiety and despair, and finally, at its worst, terrifying feelings of the impending doom of personal disintegration.

It was, of course, the onset of clinical depression. Its causes were manifold: intense academic pressures; having to work half-time while pursuing full-time studies; responsibilities as a husband and the father of a two-year-old son plus a second child on the way (our beautiful, strawberry-blonde Elizabeth, a joy and a blessing then and now); and the loss of my fulfilling life as pastor of a close-knit and loving faith community. With the help of psychotherapy and anti-depressants, plus some intuitive remedies of my own devising such as aerobic exercise and immersion in nature, along with the support of my dear Jan for whom all this was also an awful ordeal, I was able to hang on and see it through a difficult four-year period covering the completion of required coursework, passage of qualifying exams, and the beginnings (with an initial false start) of dissertation research.

A painful crisis of faith was also involved here, a dark night of the soul. Previously I had thought that I had it pretty much all worked out, basically all thought through. But now it seemed to be unraveling, prior certainties dissolving. Had I given too much credence to the revered, all-male, neo-orthodox authority figures of the forties, fifties and early sixties —giants who, by the late sixties, were already toppling from their heights in theological academia? Had I put too much emphasis on an authoritarian, patriarchal sort of God, out there, up there, far above and beyond? If so . . . then where to turn? If not *out there* . . . then maybe *in here*? Maybe my own spiritual experience and inner life had something to offer? Maybe there was more within me, within us all—more than that line from John Watts's famous hymn suggests, "my sinful self my only shame . . ."? Maybe the Quakers were on to something about the inner light, within us all?

In the first year of this awful journey through depression, another source of healing reached out and spoke to me intuitively. It called to me from where it was hanging, displayed on the wall of a department store in Harvard Square. It was an image imprinted on a rectangular piece of fabric, four by five feet, a mesmerizing design in browns and greens and yellows with a brilliant bright circle radiating from the center, all this within a field of millions of points of light evoking the cosmos. Though it did not initially occur to me, over time I would come to see this image as a cross-section of John's organic vine-and-branches image. At first, however, it simply spoke to me, saying, "I am yours. Take me home."

Only some time later did I learn to identify this design as a mandala, an eastern religious symbol representing the cosmos, used as an object to focus attention for meditation. In Christianity, icons and rose windows have served the same spiritual purpose. At the center of a rose window, there is often Christ or Mother Mary with the infant Jesus. At the center of my mandala there is that bright, radiating golden orb that for me came to represent Christ at the center of the interconnected cosmos . . . and at the re-integrating center of my own truest and most whole self as well.

Karl Jung, who became fascinated with circles and mandalas, noted, "Only gradually did I discover what the mandala really is: . . . the Self, the wholeness of the personality, which if all goes well is harmonious."[6] Furthermore, Jung came to realize that an individual's impulse to create mandalas occurs during times of deep inner reordering and rebalancing, when profound personal growth is emerging, resulting in a more complex and better-integrated personality, in wholeness. Ever since that time when, in the midst of my own dark time of disorder and imbalance fifty years ago, I took that mandala home with me, it has hung over my desk. And when I've preached on John's vine and branches verses, it has also hung from my pulpit.

For many years now I have treasured another object as well, displayed as close as possible to my mandala. It is a copy of verses, written in calligraphy and framed in the same green and brown earth colors as the mandala, from the much longer piece known as St. Patrick's Breastplate:

> Christ be with me,
>   Christ within me,
> Christ behind me,
>   Christ before me,
> Christ beside me,
>   Christ to win me,

6. Jung, *Memories*, 195–196.

Christ to comfort
and restore me . . . (italics added)

But how, exactly, is all this related to our salvation? How does Christ restore us? Has the incarnation alone—God's assumption of our human nature in Christ, the New Adam—accomplished this, fully restoring us to our original nature as creatures made in the image of God? What place, if any, does Christ's death on the cross play in the restoration of our true nature as daughters and sons of God, destined as we are for *theosis*, deification, reunion with God?

CHAPTER 11

The Great Crossing . . .
The Great Restoration

OVER THE PAST SEVERAL decades so many progressive Christian thinkers have raised so many critical problems with traditional theories of the cross and atonement that one must wonder if the cross is now lost to progressive Christianity. Felten and Procter-Murphy approvingly quote Bishop John Shelby Spong, one of the most influential of all progressive Christian writers and lecturers, who has put it in words that could not possibly be more emphatic:

> Jesus did not die for your sins; let that be said a thousand times. Jesus did not come from God to rescue fallen, sinful, inadequate, incompetent people like you and me. That is an image of a God who comes to us from outside to rescue this terrible and fallen creation.[1]

The penal substitutionary theory of atonement, often attributed to Anselm (1033–1109) in his *Cur Deus Homo,* has come under the harshest criticism. How, ask the critics, can it be either just or loving that an otherwise just and loving God would send an innocent son to suffer and die on the cross in order to satisfy God's demands for sin's punishment? Doesn't this whole scheme of atonement rest upon a repugnant act of criminal abuse, even outright filicide by God? Furthermore, by elevating deadly scapegoating to a holy plan of salvation, doesn't this traditional thinking

---

1. Quoted by Felten and Procter-Murphy, *Living the Questions,* chapter 11.

about the cross actually condone and perpetuate the continuation of violent scapegoating throughout human history?

So, then, must we now jettison more than two thousand years of Christian Scripture and tradition regarding the cross? The critics will object that it's only a thousand years of tradition we're dealing with, since the penal substitutionary theory of atonement came to the fore only with Anselm. However, as we have previously asked, should we assume that the suffering servant verses of Isaiah 53 did not come to Jesus's mind and heart as he pondered the likely end of his ministry? Jesus, who was so steeped in Scripture, especially in the book of Isaiah upon which he drew, according to Luke, to set forth the very essence of his Spirit-anointed ministry as the servant of the Lord (Luke 4:16–21)—did it not occur to Jesus at the end of his days that he was also finally called upon to fulfill the suffering servant role defined by Isaiah (chapter 53) as the one who was to bear our griefs and carry our sorrows . . . to be wounded for our transgressions and bruised for our iniquities . . . to be the one upon whom was to be laid the suffering that makes us whole and by whose pains we are healed?

It is the long-held predominant view of mainstream New Testament scholars that this interpretation of the meaning of Jesus's death was a creation of the early church, read back into the Gospel records. But Daniel Boyarin, as emphatically as Spong, demurs:

> This commonplace view has to be rejected completely. The notion of the humiliated and suffering Messiah was not at all alien within Judaism before Jesus' advent, and it remained current among Jews well into the future following that . . .[2]

According to Boyarin, there is

> . . . a very strong textual base for the view that the suffering Messiah is based in deeply rooted Jewish texts early and late. Jews, it seems, had no difficulty whatever with understanding a Messiah who would vicariously suffer to redeem the world. Once again, what has been allegedly ascribed to Jesus after the fact is, in fact, a piece of entrenched messianic speculation and expectation that was current before Jesus came into the world at all. That the Messiah would suffer and be humiliated was something Jews learned from close reading of the biblical texts . . .[3]

2. Boyarin, *Jewish Gospels*, chapter 4.

3. Ibid., chapter 4.

In addition, of course, we have the many cross-centered proclamations of Paul, who gives us the very earliest of all written Christian testimonies: "The message about the cross . . . to us who are being saved it is the power of God" (1 Cor 1:18) and "We proclaim Christ crucified . . ." (1 Cor 1:23) and "I decided to know nothing among you except Jesus Christ, and him crucified" (1 Cor 2:2) and "May I never boast of anything except in the cross of our Lord Jesus Christ . . ." (Gal 6:14). And, too, there is the fact that, beginning with Mark, the earliest of the gospels, all four gospels devote a plurality of their records to Jesus's final days and death.

Having rejected penal substitutionary theory, must progressive Christians also reject any convincing place for a cross-centered notion of salvation that goes back to earliest Christian faith? Ever since researching the question as a student at Harvard in the early 1960s, I have been convinced that there is a view, rooted in Scripture and tradition, offering an approach that is much less problematic, far more positive and comprehensive in scope, than penal substitutionary theory. This alternative understanding of the divine will and redemptive plan emphasizes *restorative justice rather than punitive justice*, working through a Christ-centered process of *participation rather than substitution*.

This view has been persuasively articulated by Derek Flood in his grace-filled book *Healing the Gospel: A Radical Vision for Grace, Justice, and the Cross.* Flood states clearly that this approach, found in Paul and essential for Calvin, is really nothing new or innovative. Still more recently we have been blessed with Fleming Rutledge's massive, majestic, and thoroughly orthodox work, *The Crucifixion: Understanding the Death of Jesus Christ.* Rutledge's work—also finding its roots in Paul, in the early church fathers, and in Calvin—emphasizes themes of Christ's identification with humanity in biblical and classical terms of "participation," "incorporation," and "recapitulation." While she even makes a persuasive case for the notion of "substitution," I am personally convinced that that word carries too much freight of historical misinterpretation and distortion to be any longer helpful or useful pastorally or apologetically.

Rutledge concludes her sympathetic treatment of Anselm by interpreting his concept of the "satisfaction" of God's justice through Christ's death on the cross as "'reparation,' 'restitution,'—or 'rectification,' the word preferred throughout these pages."[4] For Rutledge, it all comes down to the

---

4. Rutledge, Crucifixion, 166. (Emphasis is Rutledge's)

fact that *"Something is wrong and must be put right"*[5] and *"God's powerful activity of making right what is wrong in the world."*[6] "Rectification" is Rutledge's translation of choice for "justification." I prefer with Flood to use the more accessible terms (to contemporary ears) "restoration" and "restorative justice" to describe the aim of God's saving work through Christ's death and resurrection.

For Paul, Christ is God's New Adam (Rom 5:11–21), the divine representative and embodiment of our restored humanity. He comes to us from God as one of us, a divine participant in our human nature whose work is to embody the restoration of our humanity to God's original intention. First our redeemer descends . . . then he ascends (Phil 2:1–11). This is the process and pattern of humanity's re-creation—a divine descent in human form, into and through the abyss of horribly painful and ignominious death on a cross, then ascent up and out into blessedness, exaltation, and glory on the other side. It is the great redemptive passage of restoration, a great crossing from God's side to ours and then back again.

But why is the cross necessary? Why isn't the incarnation of God in the humanity of Christ sufficient to restore us to our true nature? Because to carry us back to God's side as the agent of our restoration, Christ must engage in *the work of our re-creation.* This entails his making that great crossing, plunging into that deep, dark, watery abyss of our alienation—alienation from God, from one another, from our own truest and best selves—in order then to carry us in him, with him, and through him back to God's side.

He must bear the suffering of our alienation. Why? It is not so much a matter of divine punishment as it is the very nature of things in a moral universe. As anyone passing from addiction to recovery knows all too well, there is no way out but through. It is a painful passage requiring the recognition of pain inflicted upon self and others. The pain must be acknowledged, endured, borne. Christ bears this for us and ahead of us, not that we might be spared, but that we might then be enabled in Christ and through Christ and with Christ to make that crossing ourselves as well. This is no mere easy forgiveness from God's side. Nor is it an easy self-improvement project from our side. Nothing less is involved here than the painful work of re-creating our humanity, a work that God alone can initiate, yet one in which we must also participate.

5. Ibid., 166. (Emphasis is Rutledge's).

6. Ibid., 328.

Again, should we say that Christ on the cross is suffering for us, in our stead, God's *punishment* of our sin? Better to say, I believe, that Christ is bearing for us *the inevitable consequences* of sin, inevitable in a moral universe. Yes, this does entail the righteous judgment of a righteous God upon our human alienation from God and neighbor. This judgment is required; it is necessary because God's forgiveness is neither a mere indifference nor a permissive indulgence. God's judgment is about *restoration* and *justice*. Pain, suffering, and death are involved, but when all is said and done God's purpose is not punishment. God's merciful, redemptive judgment revealed through Christ's cross and resurrection is about setting us and all things right.

For Paul, Christ does this redeeming, restoring, reconciling work not that we might simply stand at the foot of the cross in awe-struck, grateful faith—a passive role in which the traditional emphasis on substitution tends to place us. It is, rather, that we might participate, might join Christ in his saving work of restoring our true humanity. Christ represents who we, by God's grace, are to become. Christ does what we, by God's grace, are also to do. Christ is neither God's scapegoat nor our substitute. Christ is us. He bears us in him, with him, and through him—on the cross and beyond.

We are called to embody and enact the sacred work of humanity's restoration in Christ. Rather than being mere spectators of the divine drama of cross and resurrection, we are called to become actors on the stage. Baptism is the initiating rite by which we become incorporated into Christ and his saving work (Rom 6:1–4). By the grace of God, empowered by the Spirit, we take that plunge with Christ—our own spiritual death, burial, and resurrection through those dark waters, taking on our own cross, making our own crossing that will lead us into new life.

So this is not just about God absolving us or forgiving us. This is a profoundly life-transforming process that bears concrete moral and ethical implications. It is about, as Paul says in Philippians 2, our coming to have within us the same mind that was in Christ, his disposition of humble, loving, self-offering service. It is about dying to our old selves, our self-centered, egocentric selves, so that we might be borne up and out of those waters of death into new selves, God-centered and neighbor-centered selves.

We are called into this great crossing continually, not only in our baptism, but also at the Lord's Table. In this sacrament, in Paul's words, we present our very selves "as a living sacrifice, holy and acceptable to God," which is the essence of our "spiritual worship." (Rom 12:1) In union with

Christ's offering of himself to God, we then receive ourselves back again, blessed, renewed, and transformed in the power of his resurrection to continue this sacred path throughout the course of our lives. These are not just words, not just doctrinal and sacramental abstractions. This is, as Paul makes clear in the rest of Romans 12, about our very lives, our Christian path, our dying and rising with Christ over and over. Time and again, in many various and individual ways, God calls us and enables us to let go, to relinquish, to die to old things in order to be raised up to new things.

In my Personal Prelude to this book, I have related how my teenage spiritual experience was just this sort of dying and rising experience, and an introduction to a lifetime of ongoing transformation. So also my struggle with depression in my late twenties and early thirties, which I recounted in the previous chapter, was, over a period of years, an intensely painful dying to old ideas, attitudes, and dispositions, slowly making way for new ones to be born. Chief among these was finding God within me, not just above me and beyond me. But there were also many other marvelous new gifts with which I was eventually blessed as I came through and out the other side of that pit of despair:

- Finding a new calling in Henri Nouwen's deeply affective image of Christ as *The Wounded Healer* who bids us join him in this unique sort of vulnerable, pain-sharing ministry;

- Discovering that the experience of one's own pain can undercut judgmentalism, giving birth to a deeper empathy for others in their suffering, coupled with an increasing affinity with Christian universalism—the conviction that a loving God will redeem all souls, all things;

- Claiming, beyond preaching and teaching, a ministry of listening;

- Embracing Christ as an androgynous representation of God as our Mother/Father, our Good Shepherd King, our humble and nurturing Sovereign;

- Experiencing the healing power of nature by learning the names of trees, recognizing them on long walks in the woods as new-found friends, one by one;

- Coming to a greater appreciation for both/and rather than either/or thinking;

- Reclaiming the transformational spiritual experience of my youth and renewing my commitment to spiritual disciplines.

"So if anyone is in Christ," declares Paul, "there is a new creation: everything old has passed away; see, everything has become new!" (2 Cor 5:17). For Paul and for Calvin[7] our incorporation into Christ and our participation (*koinonia*) in his life, death, and resurrection are absolutely central. Christ is not merely a substitute, standing in our stead before God, leaving us to be mere passive recipients of salvation. Christ leads the way; Christ is the way into which we are called to follow, both sacramentally and ethically. Just as cross and resurrection are indissolubly linked in the saving work of God in Christ, so are our justification by grace through faith and the lifelong process of our sanctification by the Holy Spirit. The fruit of it all is an active, activist faith, inspired by love and gratitude, transforming self and society.

This way of telling the story surely places the cross at the center of God's redeeming/restoring work in Christ. But unlike so much of penal substitutionary thinking, this understanding of the cross does not displace the salvific significance of Christ's life: his teachings, his works of merciful service and deliverance, his death as a courageous prophet who spoke truth to power and died faithful to the claim of the kingdom he proclaimed. If God in Christ has come to restore human nature, then the life he lived, the values he taught and embodied and for which he died are an essential part of his work of human restoration. The incarnation is necessary, certainly that he might die for us the death we are also called to die in him, but also that he might live for us the life that we are called to live in him.

Christ's entire life, culminating in his cross, is an offering to God of the restored humanity God wants from each of us—a life given fully to God and neighbor. As the Rev. Wallace Adams-Riley, Rector of St. Paul's Episcopal Church in Richmond, Virginia, has put it,

> . . . through the Cross, Jesus shows us what it looks like to give ourselves over to, to join in on, what God is up to in the world: To offer ourselves. To be vulnerable. To risk. To give up control. To be willing to suffer. To participate in God's reconciling, healing, hope-inducing, liberating work in the world, even while it may well and eventually surely will cost us.[8]

Anselm was rightly concerned with the absolute seriousness of sin and about God's justice being satisfied in dealing with it. If justice, however, is ultimately about setting things right, then we can surely see God's merciful

7. See Billings, *Calvin*, for a thorough treatment of this subject in Calvin's thought.

8. Adams-Riley, *The Epistle*.

restorative justice fulfilled in this telling of the story of redemption. Yes, it is indeed a painful course as it leads through the cross. But then it is through participating in Christ's offering of his redeeming life, death, and resurrection that we are carried by the Spirit into the new life and ultimately into the glory of our fully restored humanity that has always, from the very beginning, been God's destiny for us. Thus, according to Paul, we human creatures who were first fashioned in the divine image, who in Christ find ourselves being refashioned into that very same divine nature (2 Cor. 3:18), now await our ultimate glorious revealing as God's beloved sons and daughters (Rom 8:19). And not only we human beings, declares Paul, but all of creation is destined to participate in this glorious restoration of God's good intent for all things (Rom 8:19–23).

CHAPTER 12

To Embody the Good News

EVANGELISM, SPREADING THE GOSPEL, "witnessing—winning souls for Christ" is essential for evangelical Christians, but for progressive/mainline Christians it is often problematic, even suspect. Why? There are several interrelated reasons. First of all, many of us have experienced certain fervent evangelicals coming at us with "good news" in a way that makes us want to turn and run the other way. Second, evangelicals share a conviction that non-evangelicals would usually question or at least qualify—that Christ is the only way to God. Third, because of their conviction that accepting Christ is the one and only way to God, to salvation, to avoid eternal damnation, evangelicals typically have a sense of personal urgency about sharing their faith that other Christians often lack. Fourth, because evangelicals often tend to reduce the notion of salvation to a simple formula of accepting Jesus as one's personal Lord and Savior, they find it far easier to state and share their faith than do Christians who hold more complex, nuanced views. Evangelicals, of course, may respond that progressive/mainline Christians are simply uncommitted and uncertain about what they believe, even about whether or not it really matters.

As a conservative progressive Christian—one with admittedly nuanced views about salvation and Christ as the only way—I have a passion for evangelism. In the introduction to my book, *Transforming the Mainline Church*, I wrote:

> Though the word "evangelism" seldom appears in these pages, I believe that this entire book can easily be read as a book about effective evangelism . . . about the kind of evangelism that Jesus practiced, an evangelism focused primarily on reaching those

outside the faith community, those rejected and turned off by the traditional religious institutions. It is about an evangelism that is communicated as much in deeds as in words, especially in deeds of compassion, deliverance, healing, and social transformation, what we might call "incarnational evangelism."[1]

Michael Gorman makes a beautiful, persuasive case for this broader, more nuanced view of evangelism in his *Becoming the Gospel: Paul, Participation and Mission.* In his introduction Gorman sets forth a succinct statement of his position in a summary that also references several of the themes of the present book:

> The goal of human existence, for Paul and for those who receive his words as Christian Scripture, is to participate now and forever, individually and corporately, in the very life and character of this cruciform, missional, world-redeeming God of righteousness and restorative justice (*dikaiosynē*). . . . Paul believed himself to be caught up in a divine mission . . . —to spread a powerful word of good news (the "gospel") that would establish an international network of transformed, peaceable, multicultural communities worshiping, obeying, and bearing public witness to the one true God by conformity to his Son in the power of the Spirit.[2]

By and large, Gorman prefers the term "mission" to "evangelism" because, I suspect, it communicates a broader view of salvation and of what is entailed in sharing the gospel, broader than winning souls for Christ and recruiting new believers. He approvingly quotes a statement by John Wesley that all evangelicals might well commit to memory:

> By salvation I mean, not [merely] . . . deliverance from hell, or going to heaven, but a present deliverance from sin, a restoration of the soul to its primitive health, its original purity; a recovery of the divine nature; the renewal of our souls after the image of God in righteousness and true holiness, in justice, mercy, and truth.[3]

Previously, I have written of our calling to become a "Whole Gospel Church," embodying Christ's command to love God with all our heart, mind, soul, and strength—and our neighbors as ourselves:

---

1. Chesnut, *Transforming,* 5–6.
2. Gorman, *Becoming the Gospel,* "Invitation."
3. Ibid., "Invitation," Quoted from Cragg, *Works of John Wesley,* 106.

A Whole Gospel Church is a both/and church, a church that makes no false distinctions between individual salvation and the social gospel, no false distinctions between evangelism and social action, no false distinctions between spirituality and social justice, no false distinctions between a faith for the head and a faith for the heart. Whole Gospel vision calls us to a faith that gives equal weight to . . . our energetic action to shape that peaceful, compassionate, and just society toward which Jesus was always pointing—that realm of *shalom*, of comprehensive well-being where God's will is done on earth as it is in heaven.[4]

Furthermore:

We are called and anointed in the power of the Holy Spirit, just as Christ was, to proclaim and to practice divine deliverance for all who are enslaved, imprisoned, exploited, and oppressed. This means confronting evil spirits and evil systems, principalities and powers of many and various sorts: unjust and oppressive political and economic systems, the addictive power of drugs and alcohol, a sex- and violence-purveying entertainment industry, the meaninglessness of a life without higher purposes, materialism, racism, sexism, repressive fundamentalisms, and so on.[5]

This is the life, the mission into which we are baptized, even as we are baptized into Christ. So this is not only a matter of following the example of Jesus, of having the same mission as Jesus. This is, as Gorman maintains is the case for Paul, a matter of *becoming the gospel*—in Christ, with Christ, and through Christ. The *theosis* theme which we have previously explored—participation, being in Christ and Christ being in us—is central here. As we are incorporated into Christ, as we participate in the very *being* of Christ, so we are incorporated into and so we participate in the very *doing* of Christ, the work of Christ. With Christ and in Christ and through Christ, we ourselves become the active incarnation of the good news of God's redeeming, restoring, justice-making, right-setting, *shalom*-creating love.

Evangelism/mission is not optional for Christians and Christian congregations. Christians and churches without it are oxymoronic, a contradiction in terms. By its very nature the gospel is a gift to be embodied, passed on and shared. In Matthew's gospel Jesus makes this unmistakably

---

4. Chesnut, *Transforming*, 157–158.

5. Ibid., 157.

clear in his parable of the talents (Matt 25:19–30). Speaking to his disciples on the eve of his death and physical departure from the earth, Jesus tells of a master who, as he prepares to depart on a journey, entrusts treasure to his servants. Upon his return, the master clearly expects his servants to have acted as venture capitalists with their stewardship. The faithful servants who are rewarded are those who have taken the treasure entrusted to them and invested it, risked it, increased it, and multiplied it. The faithless servant is the one who was afraid of doing anything with it and so simply buried it in the ground for safekeeping. So, as Jesus hands over his mission and ministry on earth to his disciples, he is telling them that the gospel of God's love must, by its very nature, be taken out into the world to be shared. This is the essence of love. It cannot be hoarded. It is only possessed as it is shared. To have it is to give it. We use it or we lose it.

Matthew's risen Christ delivers the same charge to his disciples, his very last words in what we call his "Great Commission"—"Go therefore and make disciples of all nations, baptizing them in the name of the Father and of the Son and of the Holy Spirit, and teaching them to obey everything I have commanded you. And remember, I am with you always, to the end of the age" (28:19–20).

But hold on. Didn't we just declare that our mission is about more than making new disciples? Yes, and Matthew's Christ affirms that as well. His parable of the talents is followed immediately by his account of the standards that the Son of Man will apply at the last judgment: Did you feed the hungry, welcome the stranger, clothe the naked, visit the sick and imprisoned (28:31–46)? Our mission is a both/and, not an either/or, affair. It is both about winning new disciples and about proclaiming the good news in word and deed, incarnating the gospel of God's redeeming love revealed in Christ through compassionate service and prophetic witness to God's reign.

Jesus Christ, according to the gospel of John, is the eternal Word of God who took on our flesh and dwelt among us, full of God's grace and truth and glory (John 1:1–17). This is an indwelling of the divine nature that is shared with us as well, as Christ has come to give us this divine grace (1:16) and the power to become children of God (1:12). But this is not only about our sharing in the *being* of God; it is about sharing in the *doing* of God, the work of God, the mission of God in Christ. So John's Christ says that as we abide in him, just as branches abide in the vine, we will by the very nature of that relationship bear much fruit, fruit that is manifest in love (15:1–17).

This, then, is God's plan. The Word of God's redeeming, restoring love is to become incarnate: first in Christ, then in us. From the very beginning of my ministry, over half a century ago, I have been convinced of this. Congregations make a sad, tragic mistake if, when searching for a pastor, they look first and foremost for an impressive "pulpiteer." Yes, of course, proclaiming the word is essential. Faithful, inspiring, intelligent preaching is essential. Yet if that preaching is to bear any fruit, it must be indissolubly linked to a pastor's ability to inspire and lead a congregation to embody the gospel both within its own life and for the sake of the wider community and world it is called to serve.

What will it entail? What will it look like—a faithful embodied witness to the gospel of Christ? As I near the end of my eighth decade of life, few things provide more gratification than contemplating the ongoing faithful witness of congregations that Jan and I have served with through the years, as well as those with which we have been affiliated in our retirement. Examples abound of how they have each in their own context incarnated the good news. The one I will lift up here, however, is the one we served longest of all and last of all—East Liberty Presbyterian Church in Pittsburgh (ELPC).

I will share some of what stands out in the Summer 2016 issue of the ELPC newsletter, aptly titled *Reaching Out*. First, there is a message from the Pastor, the Rev. Dr. Randy Bush, focusing on issues of economic justice. He declares that, in the Bible,

> The poor are never condemned, but instead are named as fellow human beings who need to be spared, defended and delivered. . . . We should give the needs of the poor priority over the arguments, tax code machinations, and political rhetoric associated with the most wealthy. There is a place for both groups in God's Kingdom, but in terms of biblical justice, the conversations will always be biased towards the poor.

Second, in that same publication there is a note of farewell and thank you from the seminary intern who served ELPC over the previous year. He writes, "As an openly gay seminarian, finding a church community that would wholly accept me was a challenge. . . . I feel blessed to have served in a community that truly accepts all of God's beloved children." And he grounds the welcome he has experienced at ELPC in the witness that Christians are called by their faith to embody: "Hospitality always has been a Christian value, finding its roots in our Jewish heritage. Embracing the stranger, the foreigner, and the outcast is our shared calling as followers of Jesus."

This same newsletter also includes brief testimonies of faith from the seven young people recently confirmed. One states, "God calls me to care and love everyone, forgive all, and use my gifts to serve our communities and many others." Another affirms: "Through accepting Jesus's teachings and sacrifice, we allow ourselves to be molded into the people that God wants us to be." And another: "The church is the house of God, a teaching place, but most importantly, it's a place of acceptance for all."

The same issue of *Reaching Out* includes invitations to explore opportunities for welcoming refugee families with the Jewish Family and Children's Service Refugee Department; working in a nearby urban garden project; joining in the Pittsburgh Pridefest's Equality March; meditating with neighbors at the Pittsburgh Buddhist Center; studying and discussing a book that "tackles common stereotypes and misconceptions" about Islam; and supporting the congregation's new Chapel Market, which in the first ninety days of its operation distributed more than 9,400 items of donated clothing free of charge to men, women, and children in the community.

All this offers but a snapshot of a congregation that will be 200 years old in 2019. Since the end of World War II, the once all-white, upper-status congregation has experienced tremendous change in its urban neighborhood, finding itself by the 1970s and eighties in the midst of a predominantly African-American, economically distressed community. Faithfully responding to the challenge, ELPC began in the 1960s to welcome its first black members. It was instrumental in forming an interfaith coalition of congregations and synagogues to serve the community, and it has actively supported a community development corporation that has successfully worked to renew local economic opportunities and expand equal housing opportunity and home ownership.

Over the past thirty-plus years ELPC has housed a men's homeless shelter, a daily free lunch program, and after-school tutoring and recreation programs for children. The congregation has supported a nearby free health clinic, organized a performing arts academy for neighborhood children, welcomed the Pittsburgh gay men's chorus as artists in residence, and advocated for LGBT equality in the denomination and wider community. Sister parish partnerships in Guatemala and Malawi have extended the church's embodied witness of Christian compassion and justice worldwide.

One of the most impressive features of ELPC's witness to the gospel of Christ is its diverse, inclusive membership. Nationwide studies have shown that progressive/mainline congregations rank last in racial/ethical diversity behind evangelical and Roman Catholic churches. But East Liberty Presbyterian stands out in this regard, not just with its racial/ethnic diversity but also by embracing people across distinctions of social class, urban/suburban residence, generation, and sexual orientation/identity. The masthead of its publications declares: "As a diverse community of believers . . . we show God's unconditional love by providing a refuge for spiritual growth, ardently pursuing justice, and extending Christ's radical hospitality to all."

In a personal communication, Randy Bush shared further thoughts about the congregation's witness to its Christian faith:

> As you know, ELPC is a special place—not only because we can talk openly about justice issues, but also because it is always done in a context of welcome and inclusion. In terms of evangelism and ELPC, one of our strengths is that once a congregation commits to a gospel that is inclusive and just, the individual members become the best ambassadors for outreach and evangelism.
>
> Another detail I would offer is that our church's social justice perspective is tremendously attractive to young adults. This is especially true in relation to our positions on anti-racism as well as LGBTQ inclusion. We regularly have 20–30 year olds coming in who mostly did not grow up in a church, but who are aware of our advocacy and activism and decide to check out these "Presbyterians." Often we are welcoming them into a congregational community and then explaining what it means to be Presbyterian.
>
> Lastly, the way that ELPC opens the building to the community is a big part of our evangelism efforts. Evangelism is about conversations—but there is a "spatial evangelism" in which people come together and interact, out of which you can have the spiritual conversation. Too many churches insist on reversing this order—talk first about Jesus and then get them inside the doors—but for us and our myriad of offerings/events, the opposite approach has worked best.[6]

What we have here, I believe, is a congregation that exemplifies Michael Gorman's view, cited above, that Paul understood himself to be living

---

6. Personal e-mail from Randy Bush, June 30, 2016.

out a mission to "spread a powerful word of communities worshiping, obeying, and bearing public witness to the one true God by conformity to his Son in the power of the Spirit." Moreover, adds Gorman, the inherent nature of these communities would be "to participate now and forever, individually and corporately, in the very life and character of this cruciform, missional, world-redeeming God of righteousness and restorative justice (*dikaiosynē*) . . ."

Part of me hesitates to conclude this basically positive, upbeat chapter on something of a downbeat. But faithfulness to the gospel requires it. As often as not, the Bible offers us both good news and bad news . . . or at least some very challenging news. Jesus stated it succinctly with his twofold proclamation: "Repent . . . and believe the good news." So then . . . did you note the word "cruciform" in the last sentence of the paragraph above? Together with "cruciformity," that word appears no less than 100 times in Gorman's book. It points us to the Pauline notion that as we live in Christ and Christ lives in us, so we are conformed through the power of the Holy Spirit to the pattern of Christ's saving work, his death and resurrection. Again, as we have said many times, this inevitably suggests a cross-centered faith and life, a life that follows the pattern of Christ's redemptive descent and ascent as laid out in Philippians 2:5–11—the pattern of self-giving, self-sacrificing love and service to others. Moreover, this may well mean —as it did for Paul and for some of those in the congregations he established —enduring painful persecutions and even death.

The convictions and values we have celebrated above, those embodied in the life and ministry of the East Liberty Church, were at times, for those of us in the thick of it, hard-won. In many places today in our land and in our churches, they are still far from being universally affirmed. Indeed, they are often widely challenged. Christians who stand and witness for human equality across distinctions of race and class and creed and sexual orientation/identity can sometimes pay a heavy price. In the aftermath of the 2016 election, various houses of worship around the country were defaced with hateful graffiti, and even, in at least one instance, firebombed.

Thomas Friedman wrote in mid-2016 of a U.S. presidential campaign replete with bald-faced lies and blatant appeals to various sorts of bigotry, ignorance and fear. He forcefully indicted leaders who display a moral bankruptcy by caving into naked political expediency, concluding:

> This is such a pivotal moment; the world we shaped after W.W. II is going wobbly. This is a time for America to be at its best, defending

its best values, which are now under assault in so many places—pluralism, immigration, democracy, trade, the rule of law and the virtue of open societies.[7]

I have written in the Prologue about the indelible impression left by seeing in my early childhood a picture of Jesus hanging on the cross. Yet another indelible impression was made a few years later by pictures I saw in *Life* magazine at age seven. It was 1945, and these were unbelievably horrific images of huge piles of emaciated human corpses left by the Nazis as they fled concentration camps being liberated by the Allies. As I grew and as my faith grew over the years that followed, I became more and more convinced that being a Christian calls us to a faithful courage that will steel us to stand against evil—and to do so early on in the struggles of our own times, before ever again a state of affairs could arise such as the one that silent and complicit Christians allowed to develop in Nazi Germany. Moral courage, I long ago concluded, is like a muscle. It requires regular exercise or it will fail us when we need it. If we don't stand up sooner, we are not likely to stand up later.

Often in my preaching over the years I have quoted German Lutheran Pastor Martin Niemöller's famous words:

> First they came for the Socialists, and I did not speak out—
> Because I was not a Socialist.
> Then they came for the Trade Unionists, and I did not speak out—
> Because I was not a Trade Unionist.
> Then they came for the Jews, and I did not speak out—
> Because I was not a Jew.
> Then they came for me—and there was no one left to speak for me.[8]

Though initially a supporter of Hitler, as Niemöller came to realize the tragic error of that choice, he joined the Confessing Church, the Christian resistance group with which Dietrich Bonhoeffer and Karl Barth were affiliated. Bonhoeffer, of course, was executed as a result of his participation in a plot to assassinate Hitler. Niemöller spent the last seven years of the Nazi reign in prison, barely escaping execution himself.

In our churches, during the Civil Rights and Vietnam War struggles of the sixties and seventies, we sang with full-throated fervor "Once to Every

---

7. Friedman, "Dump G.O.P.," A21.

8. A wide variety of versions of this famous statement exists because Niemöller himself used different versions on different occasions. For more information see https://en.wikiquote.org/wiki/Martin_Niemöller.

Man and Nation," James Russell Lowell's poem "The Present Crisis" set to music with the stirring Welsh hymn tune *Ton-Y-Botel*. Written in 1845, the poem was a statement of inspired protest both to the Mexican-American War and to slavery. Surely Martin Luther King Jr. sang it many times, and very likely Dietrich Bonhoeffer did as well when he was a student and teaching fellow at Union Theological Seminary in New York City in the 1930s. Though the language strikes us now as somewhat stilted and archaic, the convictions are timeless and every bit as relevant in our present crisis as when they were first penned.

> Once to every man and nation
> Comes the moment to decide,
> In the strife of truth and falsehood,
> For the good or evil side;
>
> Some great cause, God's new Messiah,
> Off'ring each the bloom or blight,
> And the choice goes by forever
> 'Twixt that darkness and that light.
>
> By the light of burning martyrs,
> Jesus' bleeding feet I track,
> Toiling up new Calvaries ever
> With the cross that turns not back;
>
> New occasions teach new duties,
> Time makes ancient good uncouth;
> They must upward still and onward,
> Who would keep abreast of truth.
>
> Though the cause of evil prosper,
> Yet the truth alone is strong;
> Though her portion be the scaffold,
> And upon the throne be wrong;
>
> Yet that scaffold sways the future,
> And, behind the dim unknown,
> Standeth God within the shadow,
> Keeping watch above His own.[9]

Good news embodied? Yes! Yes—in the conviction that the scaffold, like the cross, sways the future. Yes—in the conviction that God stands within the shadow, keeping watch above his own. Yes—in the conviction shared with Martin Luther's "mighty fortress" affirmation that "The body they may kill,

9. *The Hymnal*, 373.

God's truth abideth still; his kingdom is forever." Yes—when we remember that the New Testament word for "martyr" means "witness."

CHAPTER 13

God's Kingdom Is Forever
. . . For All Souls
. . . For All Creation

IT IS A COMMON failing of evangelical Christians to make salvation all about individuals getting saved from hell and making it to heaven. This can lead to neglecting, or at best slighting, the many-faceted biblical promise of God's coming kingdom that will see the completion of Christ's comprehensive victory over sin and death, including his triumph over all the evil cosmic powers and principalities that oppress and exploit both humanity and the rest of God's good creation. The Bible promises not just personal salvation, but a new creation, a new heaven and a new earth, a cosmic restoration of God's justice and *shalom*.

On the other hand, I must also address what appears to me a common failing of many progressive Christian expectations regarding the hereafter. Assessing "the popular Christian notion of what life after death means for the individual believer," Felten and Procter-Murphy have written:

> The idea that worthy believers will somehow be resuscitated in another life is the conventional wisdom expressed at most every funeral in Western culture. Grieving loved ones, those preparing to die for a cause, or those who are forced to endure hardships in this life are assured that there is a better life somewhere beyond this mortal coil. One is hard-pressed to find any but the slimmest

support in the New Testament for our popular notions of life after death.[1]

And, they declare,

Regardless of how little biblical evidence there is for popular ideas of life after death, many people take comfort in the simplistic notion that they will somehow be with their loved ones in the next life. This idea has become so fixated in the minds of many faithful that it could often be perceived as the primary reason people claim an allegiance to Christianity. As such, it becomes a major obstacle in understanding any deeper meaning of resurrection—and to living one's life in the present. Whatever perspective one has on life after death, the eternal is not something off in some vague, unknowable, distant future. Whatever the eternal might be, it begins here as part of who we are today. The message of resurrection is new life now.[2]

In the last book he wrote before his death, *Convictions*, Marcus Borg expressed a similar view:

. . . Christianity is not primarily about heaven and hell. . . . [S]alvation in the Bible is seldom about an afterlife but mostly about transformation this side of death—not so that we can go to heaven, but because transformation in this life matters.[3]

So, in the end, Borg professes himself to be an agnostic about life after death.[4]

Now I wholeheartedly agree that a preoccupation with getting into heaven when we die has all too often distracted many Christians from their calling here and now. Our baptism—our ritual death, burial, and resurrection with Christ—inducts us into a new life, new attitudes, and new ways, here and now. To suggest, however, that this existential meaning exhausts New Testament affirmations of resurrection, renewal, and restoration does not square with the message of Jesus and the New Testament as a whole.

Again and again we have seen how the big picture of Jesus's message, indeed of the entire New Testament, is that a God of mercy and deliverance, of justice and *shalom* reigns supreme in the universe. Is this a trustworthy

1. Felten and Procter-Murphy, chapter 12.
2. Ibid, chapter 12.
3. Borg, *Convictions*, 80.
4. Ibid., 72–74.

view of ultimate reality or not? Of course this reign has not yet come fully upon the earth, but Jesus has taught his disciples to expect it, pray for it, and work for it. Martin Luther King Jr. was paraphrasing Theodore Parker, a nineteenth-century Unitarian minister who struggled against slavery, when he said, "The arc of the moral universe is long but it bends toward justice."[5] Do we believe that or not? Multiple scriptures promise that God will eventually set things right in a new world, a new life, a new dimension yet to come. Is that a false promise? Is it only an empty metaphor that points to nothing beyond itself? As I have made abundantly clear in my own teaching and preaching over many years, I could not agree more with Dale Allison at this point:

> If what we see on this earth is all that we will ever see, if there is no further repairing of wrongs beyond what we have already witnessed, then divine love and justice do not really count for much. This is not, for me, a theological cliché but a philosophical necessity. If the sufferings of the present time are never eclipsed, if there is nothing beyond tragedy and the monotony of death, then I for one do not believe that Jesus' good God exists.[6]

Allison's latest effort, *Night Comes: Death, Imagination and the Last Things*, is entirely devoted to this concern—our survival of death. The book is unflinchingly honest and intellectually wide-ranging, imminently personal and engaging. I cannot recommend it highly enough. In spite of all the biblical, philosophical, and scientific complexities he acknowledges, as a believer Allison concludes:

> There must be some analogue to this scene in the universal human story. If not, then the cosmos is finally apathetic, and death can separate us from the love of God; and if that's so, then love doesn't endure all things but finally fails. Which cannot be.[7]

In my college years I decided that I could be a Christian believer while, like Borg, remaining an agnostic about this. But many years ago I came to the same conclusion as Allison. For those of us who have led relatively comfortable lives, safe and secure lives, this life in this world may be enough without the expectation of anything beyond. But what of all the countless millions of souls whose earthly existence has been, from beginning to end,

---

5. Quoted in Warren, *King Came Preaching*, 190.

6. Allison, *Historical Christ*, 100.

7. Allison, *Night Comes*, 18.

little more than unmitigated suffering? How can we offer them Jesus's message of assurance that God aims to set things right—doing everything we can, of course, to relive suffering and redress injustice here and now—without pointing to another world beyond this? How callous is that? Doesn't it make our preaching of ultimate good news a bait-and-switch proposition, a shell game, smoke and mirrors? Now you see it; now you don't.

"For now we see in a mirror, dimly," writes Paul, "but then we will see face to face. Now I know only in part; then I will know fully, even as I have been fully known" (1 Cor. 13:12). This is indeed very intimate, personal language, suggesting the kind of relationship we may expect with our God hereafter! And it is perfectly congruent with the notion of the resurrection of the body. For what does the body represent; what does it embody? Our bodies contain and express our unique personal identity. Above all else, the resurrection of the body—as a transformed spiritual body, according to Paul (1 Cor. 15:35–55)—is about the eternal value God places on our precious individuality.

Expecting to see God face to face, expecting to see other souls face to face, is a very different notion of what we may expect hereafter than the vision traditionally offered by Hinduism and Buddhism. The extinction of the self, the merging of the self like a drop of water in the great ocean of the world soul, is what it all comes down to in the end for Eastern religion. For Christianity it is about the ultimate perfection of the beloved community into which we are called, here and now, as the body of Christ. We have considered previously the notion of *theosis,* our ultimate participation (*koinonia*) in the very being of God. But this is not total absorption into the divine; this is a communion, a loving unity with God and with others in which our precious personal identity is preserved as a part of the whole, just as it is within the body of Christ here on earth (1 Cor. 12).

So who may expect to participate in this beatific vision of the hereafter? The traditional, conservative Protestant position in its strictest expression is, to say the least, downright harsh: You must confess faith in Jesus Christ as your personal Lord and Savior before you die or you will have no chance at heaven—your soul is forever lost, damned to hell for eternity.

This confess-Christ-before-death exclusivism gives rise to some real problems. What about the infant or young child who dies before making a confession of faith? What about those who have never heard of Christ? What about those who have rejected Christ because they have heard and seen nothing but a distorted image of Christ in the words and deeds of people who profess to be Christians, yet who embody nothing of Christ's true Spirit of love? What about sincere believers of other faiths who do not profess faith in Christ, yet who actually live a more Christ-like life than many Christians? Are we really ready to think that all these persons are destined for nothing but separation from God and eternal torment? Does that seem fair or just? Is that really the kind of God Jesus would lead us to believe in, to trust? Progressive Christians would offer a resounding "NO!"

So is there any both/and approach to this, any possible middle ground that can affirm *both* that Jesus is indeed the way, the truth, and the life, *and* that all souls, in the end, *will* come to God *through Jesus*? I believe so, as I have previously detailed elsewhere.[8] Here I will expand upon those affirmations.

Jesus reveals a God who offers second chances, yea, third and fourth chances, a God who asks us to forgive again and again, as often as seventy times seven. Jesus reveals a God who seeks out lost and unlikely souls: the woman caught in adultery, the prodigal son, the tax collector, the one lost sheep out of a hundred, the lame, and the lepers. Jesus kept pushing to widen the circle, to include more and more rather than fewer and fewer souls in the embrace of God's love. That's a large part of what got him in trouble with the religious elite who wanted to keep the circle small and tight, to include just themselves and their own kind, the chosen few who met all the qualifications.

Jesus revealed God's tough love toward narrow-minded, judgmental, exclusivist, legalistic, self-righteous folks. He said to them, "Woe to you, for the harlots and tax collectors will enter the kingdom of heaven before you. Woe to you. You impose your religion on others as a heavy burden, yet you won't lift a finger to help them. You prevent others from entering God's kingdom, yet you won't go in yourselves" (paraphrased verses from Matt 23). "So the last will be first, and the first will be last" (Matt 20:16).

Jesus clearly makes this point in his parable about the landowner who pays his workers the same full daily wage no matter how many hours they worked (Matt 20:1–16). The landowner represents God and God's amazing grace, which transcends strict notions of fairness in the direction of an abundant and undeserved goodness that gives everyone equally what they need. In this case the landowner gives enough so that all the workers—even those who labored only one hour—and their families could eat that evening. He gives them their daily bread, the staff of life. But then, of

---

8. Chesnut, *Transforming*, 139–40.

course, there are those who worked the whole day who complain about this arrangement. They represent legalists who objected to Jesus's understanding of God's amazing grace, a divine generosity transcending their strict, narrow definitions of righteousness.

This widening of the circle of God's redeeming love receives universal expansion in several of the Pauline epistles. In the letter to the Colossians, the Cosmic Christ is declared to have accomplished a cosmic transformation, the reconciliation of all things to God:

> He [Jesus Christ] is the image of the invisible God, the firstborn of all creation, for in him *all things* in heaven and on earth were created, things visible and invisible, whether thrones or dominions or rulers or powers—*all things* have been created through him and for him. He himself is before *all things* and in him *all things* hold together. . . . For in him all the fullness of God was pleased to dwell, and through him God was pleased to reconcile to himself *all things*, whether on earth or in heaven, by making peace through the blood of his cross. (Col. 1:15–17, 19–20, emphasis added)

A similar affirmation is found in Ephesians, which declares that God's eternal redemptive purpose in Christ is a "plan for the fullness of time, to gather up *all things* in him, things in heaven and things on earth" (1:10, emphasis added). Likewise, a proclamation of the objective, comprehensive effect of God's redemptive work in Christ is found in Romans 5:12–21, where Paul compares the universal result of the first Adam's sin to the universal restoration wrought by Christ as the New Adam: "Therefore just as one man's trespass led to condemnation for *all*, so one man's act of righteousness [i.e., of setting things right] leads to justification [being made right] and life for *all*" (vs. 18, emphasis added). And in I Corinthians 15:22 Paul asserts that "as *all* die in Adam, so *all* will be made alive in Christ" (emphasis added).

But doesn't a belief that everyone and all things are finally redeemed undermine discipleship and morality in this life? With those day-long workers in Jesus's parable who were so offended by their employer's generosity to those who had worked far less than they had, we too might ask if the landowner's generosity was really right and fair. If we thought that we could just put in one hour of work each day, that we could simply live any way we wanted in this life and still get to heaven in the end, then why not have our cake and eat it too?

While God in Christ bears the judgment for us all, this is not a mere indulgence that simply lets us off the hook, suggesting that there is no judgment hereafter for each of us. It means that we have every good reason to expect that God's redeeming love displayed on the cross reveals that, at the last judgment, whatever each soul is going to face, God's purpose will be our restoration, our purification—our *purgation*, if you will.

Let's think of it this way: Yes, God is a God of universal grace, mercy, and forgiveness. However, God is not merely a permissive parent, indifferent to our waywardness. The cross represents, among various things, the consequence of human sin. It is the inevitable, painful result of our human alienation from God, from one another, from our own true selves. It expresses the just divine judgment inherent in a morally ordered universe. Yet it is also—in an act of incredible, amazing grace—a judgment that God took upon God's own self in Jesus Christ.

The cross reveals that God's purpose in judgment is not punitive. It is to redeem and restore, not to condemn and to destroy. What good and loving parent would ever discipline his or her children in ways that would terribly hurt or destroy them? The discipline applied by a loving parent aims to be redemptive and corrective, not merely punitive, certainly not destructive.

This is why our Christian faith that Jesus is to be our final judge is so reassuring. Jesus is the merciful, compassionate agent of God's redeeming love, even in and through divine judgment. Thus we can gladly take our stand with John's Gospel to proclaim that Jesus is the gateway to God, the Way, the Truth, and the Life; indeed, even that it is through him that all souls will come to God (John 14:6). All souls will finally come to see that the truth of God is what we see in Jesus.

This is not to say, though, that everyone who simply calls on the name of Jesus has access to the kingdom of God unavailable to those of other faiths or of no faith. We remember Jesus's warning that it is not all those who cry "Lord, Lord," but those who do the will of God who will enter the kingdom. So we may expect some surprises to come. I have long suggested that some of those who claim to know Jesus now, when they finally see him face to face, seeing the full truth of who he is and what he stands for, may have to confess, "I knew your name, but I really didn't know you or your way." Others may exclaim, "Oh, that's who you are. I knew you and your way all along. I just didn't know your name."

So imagine, if you will, that the last judgment might well go something like this. You are in a giant Omnimax theatre, seated beside Jesus, surrounded by all the people you've ever met in your life. The film showing on the wrap-around screen is the story of your life. There you see in intimate detail—sometimes in agonizing detail—your life history. You see where you have gone wrong, how you have hurt yourself and others. And, yes, you also see how you have been kind and fair, compassionate and just. The purpose of this sometimes painful process—this final judgment at the Omnimax—will be to assure that each of us fully comprehends both the wrong and the right of how we have lived, so that, as a snake sheds its skin, we can shed all that is unworthy of God and of God's eternal company. This will give us the preparatory time and insight we need to become citizens of God's heavenly kingdom.

Dale Allison documents how the last judgment has been understood as a life review in Christian thought, beginning with the early church fathers, up through Aquinas and into modern times—indeed, how the "life review" is a common theme in various religions and cultures as well as in numerous modern accounts of near-death experiences.[9] Furthermore, he sets forth his own Christian conviction that this purgative, transformative process must deal with the essential human problem of egocentricity that lies at the heart of our self-absorbed alienation from God, neighbor, and our own true selves:

> It's precisely the promise of more than death that raises the possibility of unraveling our currently constructed egos, of crucifying our self-centered perceptions, of repositioning our displaced centers. Whatever else heaven may be, surely it must be the transition from vain self-importance to disinterested love, the end of the ever-grasping self, the obliteration of I Me Mine. So although the hope for a life beyond is often an extension of self-love, an escapist indulgence, a Goldilocks tale where everything is "just right," Christians can and should imagine it to be something else. It should be the prospect, perhaps quite painful, of dismantling our egos as we have known them, for the sake of something unimaginably larger and more profound than our current individual selves. Won't the new creation require that its citizens be re-created, and that the first-person singular no longer be capitalized?[10]

9. Allison, *Night Comes*, 54–72.
10. Ibid., 80.

Thus for many souls this purgatory process of preparation for heaven may be quite difficult—more prolonged and painful for some, of course, than for others. At times some of us may feel like we're in hell as we are required to look fully and honestly at the harm we have done and the hurt we have caused, how we have failed to love mercy, to do justice, and to walk humbly with our God. So is this not an understanding of hell that is consistent with the God of Jesus, who is both just and loving? Hell is the pain a soul may feel when going through a difficult process of purgative last judgment, a process that may feel like it is lasting forever. But it will not. Hell is but a temporary state of soul, the ultimate purpose of which is redemptive, preparatory for heaven. God's final judgment is, therefore, *both* just *and* merciful.

Does this way of understanding the last judgment sound close to the Catholic concept of purgatory? It is and it isn't. You could call it a Protestant purgatory; its purpose is sanctification, transformation, not punishment. It is the way that a number of Protestant theologians have come to understand and affirm something similar to purgatory in more recent years. While the Catholic doctrine of purgatory has traditionally put far more emphasis on punishment for sin, the Protestant view would see it as a process of redemptive purification, sanctification, transformation, preparation for eternity with God. One twentieth-century Protestant thinker who came to this way of thinking about purgatory was the late great C.S. Lewis of the Anglican tradition.[11] More recently, Jerry Walls, an evangelical British Methodist theologian, has devoted his *Purgatory: The Logic of Total Transformation* to a sympathetic treatment of the topic. And a growing number of evangelical theologians have been coming to the view that there is no eternal hell, that all souls are saved in the end, or that there is at least another chance after death.[12]

This sort of universalism is not really, however, an innovative view within the history of Christian thinking. "Patristic universalism" or "purgatorial universalism" was espoused by certain of the early church fathers, such as Clement of Alexandria, Origen, and Gregory of Nyssa. This view maintains that souls still unsaved at death will undergo hell, yes; but hell is

11. Lewis, *Letters to Malcolm*, ch. 20, ¶7–12.

12. See, e.g., evangelicaluniversalist.com; Talbott, *The Inescapable Love of God*; and MacDonald, *The Evangelical Universalist*.

remedial, not everlasting and not just retributive. Even after death, conversion is possible.[13]

Still, the question arises: If we're all going to get another chance after we die, what difference does it make whether or not in this life we believe in Christ? Why should we strive to amend our ways and lead a Christian life? Why should we strive to be faithful Christians and share the good news with others?

Surely, if our Christian faith is about more than the self-centered goal of escaping hell and getting to heaven when we die, then here and now we will aim to get a head start on the kingdom of heaven. Surely, if we believe that Christ has revealed to us both our own true nature and the true nature of the God with whom we are going to spend eternity, we will want to begin now to fit ourselves for that life. Believing that Christ has revealed to us the God who reigns at the center of the cosmos, we will want to shape our lives in harmony with that cosmic goodness and beauty, truth and love.

This is the good news that we believe, that we live by, that we gladly share with others. With Christ, in Christ, through Christ we can begin here and now to comprehend who God really is, what the nature of ultimate reality is, who our own best and truest selves are. So we can begin here and now to shape lives that are centered, rooted, and grounded in divine love—knowing that, as John says, "There is no fear in love, but perfect love casts out fear; for fear has to do with punishment . . . ." (I John 4:18). This is a love that aims to set each of us and all things right, a love that will still stand when all else has fallen.

Yes, this is good news of eternal life for each and every precious soul. It is not just about getting ourselves to heaven when we die, a question that is, I believe, already settled in our favor. It is also about working with God in this life to bring heaven and earth a bit closer in our own lives and for the sake of others. It is about embodying here and now the good news of God's gracious kingdom, just as Jesus did, especially for the last and the least, the lost and the lonely.

And in the end this is, as we have seen, about more than even solely the human race. This is about the ultimate transformation of all things . . . all things in heaven and on earth . . . all things renewed . . . all things united in God. The resurrection of Christ swallows up sin and evil, death and decay. Even the material world is finally to be liberated from its bondage to corruption, set free from its groaning as if in labor to be born again. "See,"

---

13. See Hanson, *Universalism,* for a classic exploration of this subject.

says the risen, reigning, and ever-living Christ, "I am making all things new . . . a new heaven and a new earth" (Rev. 21:1, 5).

In conclusion, I offer a blessing that is my own paraphrase of Hebrews 13:20–21:

> May the God of life and love, the God of peace and power who brought again from the dead our Lord Jesus Christ, that great shepherd of the sheep, through the blood of the everlasting covenant, may that same God keep on raising us up from everything that is dead and dying to all that lives forever, working in us and through us everything that is pleasing to God, bringing us at last to our consummation in Jesus Christ our Lord to whom be all glory forever and ever.

Footprints of a Pastor[1]

HE CAME TO US for his first pastorate in July, 1962, and leaves September 1966 to return to Harvard Divinity School for studies toward a PhD in Religion and Society. In those short four years he has left well-marked footprints. They demonstrate a most emphatic conviction that the church must be relevant in time and place. A full account of the four-year trail would be tediously long—as well try to chart the course of a hummingbird! A brief sketch of his image, based on some of the well-marked heel-to-toe footprints in the record, will need to suffice. . . . The traits of his ministry establish the following viewpoints:

Christian Education Should Be Emphasized.

. . . Early in his ministry emphasis was placed on need for re-vitalizing . . . the Church School program. In the fall of 1962, a separate Sunday Church School was started, with classes for all ages, including adults. Always a teacher himself . . . with a characteristic directness, he initiated an adult Bible study course and emphasized the need for teacher preparation and training. An important supporting feature was the establishment of a church library. . . .

---

1. This statement is excerpted from one written by Elder John Wiseman of the Calvin Presbyterian Church of Withamsville-Amelia, Ohio. His tribute appeared in the Calvin Church bulletin of September 11, 1966. On February 8, 1967, the church's Session granted approval to Harvard Divinity School to reprint it for distribution to the school's alumni.

The Minister Should Be a Pastor to the Congregation.

He taught with sermons, he led us in prayer, he counseled the troubled, and visited the sick.

The Church is Ecumenical.

He served as President of the West Clermont Ministerial Association and Vice-Chairman of the Pastors' Association. A local newspaper referred to "an ecumenical first" when a Catholic layman was the speaker at a Calvin Church Reformation Sunday service. A perfect ultimate goal would be complete unity in an ecumenical church. As a practical matter, he does not see this goal in sight. He believes we should practice cooperative action in those matters on which there is unity, particularly at the local community level.

The Church Should Be Relevant to Co-existent Society.

A statement in an issue of the Harvard Divinity Newsletter is quoted in part: ". . . the kind of ministry that society now requires is a recognition that it must involve itself in the life of the church and society, must raise issues of human importance, range itself on the side of intelligent solutions, and be stirring with responses to the modern world." One could surmise that Bob Chesnut originated this philosophy, rather than that he became a follower of it.

Here Is the Record:

Pastor Chesnut joined with 11 other Clermont clergymen to mount a campaign for passage of a school bond issue for much-needed schools in the West Clermont School District and served as general chairman of the Steering Committee. The issue had failed three previous times, but passed this fourth time, in May 1964. Characteristic response to this achievement in press and radio headlines appeared like this: "When the Church Gets Relevant," "Clermont County Ministers are Doing Something about Schools," "A Magnificent Job," "History Was Made Tuesday," etc.

A social concerns committee for Clermont County, an interdenominational organization concerned with helping needy people, was organized at Calvin Church.

Civil Rights was supported in Pastor Chesnut's sermons, in guest ministers' sermons on race relations, and by speakers before church group meetings.

Civic leaders arranged a meeting to promote economic improvement in the area. Yes—Robert A. Chesnut was there, serving as chairman of the publicity committee.

Adequate local civil government, anti-poverty programs, church administration, all have received his active interest.

The Record Is Complete . . .

but mere records cannot present a complete measure of the imprints left on the hearts and minds of this community. Personality, sturdy logic, keen intellect, sound theology, a charming wife, Jan, and young son, Andrew, born during his stay here, all contribute to these indelible imprints.

We regret to see Pastor Chesnut and his family leave us. However, this regret is tempered by our gratitude for the time he has been here and our happiness at the success he will achieve elsewhere.

Two Sides of the Coin

The Rev. Robert A. Chesnut, Ph.D.

The Gayton Kirk Presbyterian Church

Henrico, Virginia

January 31, 2016

A COUPLE OF CAUTIONS before I begin: First, this is as much a teaching sermon as a preaching sermon. It may require some extra attention and some extra thought. So put on your thinking caps and stay alert. Secondly, I may say some things today that you don't agree with. That's fine, but in that case, I am going to be making you a special offer this morning. So you'll want to stay awake for that.

"There are two sides of the coin," we sometimes say. I want us to consider two sides of several coins today. First how do we understand the truth of the Bible? Then . . . how do we understand what the Bible is telling us about God's purposes, about the purpose and mission of Jesus . . . and thus our own purpose and mission as followers of Jesus? I hope this is going to help us understand what we are to be about as disciples and as citizens . . . as a church and a nation.

Sunday before last, our Pastor gave us an insightful and delightful take on how Jesus began his ministry according to the Gospel of John. It was at a wedding that Jesus and his mother Mary attended in Cana of Galilee. A wedding, of course, is a joyous celebration and nowhere more so than in the Middle East. As Janet pointed out, this event probably went on for three days.

Now the problem at this particular wedding was that the hosts had apparently not planned very well. So they ran out of wine, well before the shindig was done. Jesus's mother took note of this and called it to the attention of her son . . . with the rather clear implication that he should do something about it. And, after some initial reluctance, Jesus did just that—and how! He turned a phenomenal amount of water into a phenomenal amount of wine. And not just any old wine, but an extra-fine wine. John doesn't say so, but that party might have gone on even more than three days!

On our Communion table this morning there is a needlepoint piece given to us by our Syrian relatives. It delightfully depicts the celebration of a traditional Middle Eastern wedding, with food and dancing and the groom arriving on his prancing steed. Feel free to come up after the service and take a closer look.

Janet captured in just one word the theme that she drew from John's story about the wedding, about Jesus changing water into wine. That word is joy. Joy, joy, joy. Weddings are about joy. Wedding parties are about joy. And wine? The Psalmist says, "Thanks be to God for wine that gladdens the hearts of men." And women too, of course. Jesus was there, according to John, at the start of his ministry, to make sure that hearts were gladdened, that there was indeed an abundance of wine and an abundance of joy for all. Elsewhere in John's Gospel, Jesus says twice that his purpose in coming is that we might have joy, fullness of joy, abundance of joy. (15:11; 17:13)

Now in this morning's reading from Luke's Gospel we get an entirely different account of the beginning of Jesus's ministry. Jesus is not in Cana, but in his hometown of Nazareth. He is not at a wedding, but in the synagogue. He is not changing water to wine, but he's reading scripture. He's reading a passage from the prophet Isaiah that goes like this:

"The Spirit of the Lord is upon me, because he has anointed me to bring good news to the poor . . . release to the captives and recovery of sight to the blind, to let the oppressed go free . . ." (Luke 4:18)

Then Jesus declared to the congregation, "Today these words have been fulfilled in your hearing." Wow! In other words, Jesus is saying, "These words from Isaiah are about me. Isaiah's words define me and my mission."

So we have John's account and we have Luke's account of how Jesus began his ministry. Which one is it? They can't both be true, can they? Many of you are aware that scholars tell us that John's Gospel is the very last of the four Gospels to be written, and the very least historical of them all. Luke's account is probably closer to how it actually happened.

Now some would say that this means we should discount John's story. Some would maintain that we can't go with anything that has only a slim chance of being factual. But I don't agree. Sure, we can take Luke as being more historical. But then we can also take John as being more imaginative, more poetic, more symbolic and metaphorical. It doesn't have to be either/or. It can be both/and. Both Luke and John. Both historical truth and symbolic truth. These are two sides of the coin about how we understand the truth of God's word.

Luke's account is the one before us this morning, so let's take a closer look. Obviously, this passage is of utmost importance for us, because if Jesus is telling us here what his own mission is, then he is also telling us what our mission is: To offer good news to the poor, release to the captives, sight to the blind, deliverance for the oppressed.

Some biblical background here will help us to understand why Jesus chose this particular passage from Isaiah to define his mission. Some of you know that a small group of us have been meeting to read and discuss Jim Wallis's book, *On God's Side*. Wallis says that the Bible gives us two basic, straightforward convictions. The first side of this coin of biblical conviction is that we are all, each and every one of us, children of God. Because we are created in the image of God, each and every one of us is of equal worth and value. The second side of the coin here is the basic biblical conviction that we are created not just for ourselves, but God and for one another. We are created for community . . . community with God and with one another.

So then, if this is where God is coming from, it explains where Jesus is coming from. It explains why he identified his mission as he did. If everyone is of equal worth and value in the eyes of God, God is naturally going to have a special concern for those who are not being treated like they are of equal worth and value, not being treated like they are children of God. God therefore is going to be concerned to set things right, to deliver the Hebrews from slavery in Egypt—indeed, in all times and places to deliver the oppressed, set free the captives, and bring good news to the poor. So this clearly becomes Jesus's mission. And this clearly becomes our mission too.

Really, when you think about it, what Jesus said his mission is about is close to what we affirm America is about when we pledge our allegiance to "one nation, under God, with liberty and justice for all." What we are to be about as disciples is also what we are to be about as citizens—liberty and justice for all.

Susanna Wesley was the mother of John Wesley, founder of the Methodist Church back in the 1700s. Now Susanna was the mother of 19 children in all. She was once asked which one she loved the most. And she replied, "The one who's sick until he's well . . . the one who's away until she's home." In a nutshell, I think this tells us how God loves—with special attention for those needing special attention, with special concern for those who are sick or lost and wandering from home, those not getting a fair shake, those who are being left out or put down. When some of God's children are not being treated like they are of equal worth and value, then things need to be set right. That's God's mission. That's Jesus's mission. That's our mission.

But just how are we to accomplish this mission? Here again, we face two sides of the coin. Some might say it's an either/or choice. Suppose someone stands up over here this morning and says, "The things Jesus said he was to do and we are to do—these are the very things that we are doing through the Kirk's various missions of mercy and compassion, programs that feed the hungry, provide shelter for homeless folks, and various forms of practical assistance to those in need and distress. This is what God calls us to do. This is what we are doing. It is really all we can do." I'm thinking many heads would nod in agreement.

But then suppose someone else across the room stands up and says something like this: "These programs of mercy and compassion and assistance are all well and good. But they're really just a drop in the bucket. Maybe they're just Band-Aids, even a distraction, unless we tackle systemic problems that put people in situations of need in the first place. What good does it do if we support these missions of mercy but then go off to the polls and elect people who only make matters worse for most people, elect politicians who won't support a living wage that allows working people to care for themselves and their families, politicians who have been bought off by wealthy interests to syphon off our wealth with tax breaks for those at the very top, kicking the props out from under those already struggling to keep their heads above water." How many heads would nod?

Once again, I say there are two sides of this coin. One side is that as Christians we must be responding here and now with mercy and compassion to help neighbors in need. The other side is that we must also be tackling the problems in our systems that help create those needs to begin with. It's both/and, not either/or. So in Jesus's name we act with compassion to assist neighbors in need right around us. And in the name of the kingdom Jesus taught us to pray for, we act as citizens with justice to deliver neighbors who are being crushed by systems that unfairly favor the rich and powerful.

I believe Jim Wallis is right when he says that we have two basic biblical convictions to guide us as disciples and as citizens: (1) We are all created in the image of God, all of equal worth and value; (2) We were created not just for ourselves alone but for each other. We were created for community with God and one another.

So let's look at these two affirmations as consisting of yet one more both/and proposition this morning, two more sides of one coin. First, we are each one of us a child of God, each one of us of equal worth and value. This affirmation underlies the individualism important to us as Americans. Affirming the individual is the foundation of our democracy and our free enterprise system. Everyone counts. One man, one woman, one vote. We each have a voice; freedom of speech and expression. Individual freedom to choose our faith, or no faith at all. Individual rights. We stand on our own two feet. Self-reliance. Self-determination. Individually making the most of what we've been given, being energetic, hard-working, innovative, entrepreneurial. Or . . . being a slacker, if that's your choice.

Individualism is one side of the coin. The second side of the coin is that we are not created for ourselves alone. We are created for community with God and one another. Jesus tells us to love our neighbors as ourselves, to do unto others as we would have them do unto us. Paul tells us in our reading from I Corinthians this morning that we exist only as members of one another; like different organs in one body, we simply can't live without each other. Consequently, if one is hurt, all are hurt. Community is the other side of this coin.

This communal conviction of our American heritage is expressed in the Latin phrase *e pluribus unum*. Many yet one. Unity in diversity. As a society, as a nation, we are members of one body. For me there is another beautiful expression for this conviction in our national lexicon. It is simply one word: Commonwealth. The Commonwealth of Virginia. The Commonwealth of Pennsylvania. The Commonwealth of Massachusetts. You know about the famous Boston Commons, the historic central park of downtown Boston. It's called the commons because it was originally the shared land where any and all were free to come and graze their cows, a part of the common wealth, the shared treasure.

Where is our commonwealth today? It is our public parks and public schools and public libraries; our fire and police protection; our roads and bridges. It is our army, navy, and air force; our Social Security and Medicare and Medicaid and welfare safety nets. It is our National Institutes of Health and Centers for Disease Control; our agencies that inspect and assure the safety of our foods and drugs; it is the folks who spray for mosquitoes and inspect buildings and control air traffic and try to regulate Wall Street and huge corporations, many of which are larger and more powerful than entire governments elsewhere in the world. There are, of course, many problems and imperfections in all these programs, but if cutting taxes is really all we care about, then we threaten to undermine so much of our essential, invaluable commonwealth.

What concerns Jim Wallis also concerns many of the rest of us. There are just so many loud, strident voices today advocating for just one side of this coin. They represent a hyper-individualism that does threaten to deny and decimate our commonwealth. It's all about "me," not about "we." When this extreme individualism gets expressed in economic philosophy it translates into the law of the jungle. Our economic life becomes dog-eat-dog with the devil taking the hindmost. The result is a society in which only the top dogs rule and the rest of us are lucky to get a few leftovers, fewer and fewer leftovers. It truly astounds and amazes me that we have prominent political leaders who espouse such a philosophy while at the same making loud claims to be disciples of Jesus Christ. So here's my offer this morning: If anyone could explain to me how on earth it is possible to reconcile the two sides of that coin—the way of Jesus and the law of the jungle—I will gladly sit and listen, over a free lunch that I will pay for . . . maybe in more ways than one!

Well, I know I may be on the brink of getting into trouble here. My dear wife has reminded me that in the verses in Luke that follow our reading this morning, Jesus literally finds himself on the brink. He gets run out of town . . . and very nearly pushed over the edge of a cliff for what he said in the synagogue.

I think it's time for a joke. It's an old one, what my wife likes to call one of my "old chestnuts." It takes place in a country church, probably not in Virginia or any other tobacco state, for the preacher here is railing against the evils of tobacco. "Those who smoke cigarettes and cigars are going to burn in hell," he declares. An older woman on the back bench shouts, "Preach it, brother." "Those who smoke pipes," proclaims the preacher, "will go up in smoke with the Devil!" "Amen; praise the Lord," responds the octogenarian. Then from the preacher she hears this: "Those who use snuff will be snuffed out for all eternity!" So she turns to her neighbor on the back bench and protests in a loud whisper, "Now he's stopped preaching and started meddling!"

Ultimately, it's up to each listener to decide what's preaching and what's meddling. Personally, I have no trouble concluding that Jesus, like the prophets before him, was both a preacher and a meddler. And it turns out after all, doesn't it, that that meddling country preacher was right. After half a century of medical warnings, close to half a million Americans still die annually from cigarette smoking . . . and that's not including the smoke-less stuff like chewing tobacco and snuff.

In conclusion let's do a quick recap of the two sides of several coins that we've looked at this morning:

First, there are the two sides of the coin of biblical truth. There's factual, historical truth. There's symbolic, metaphorical truth. It's both/and. Both help us understand God's word.

Next there are the two sides of the coin of Jesus's mission. John says Jesus has come to bring an abundance of joy for everyone. Luke says Jesus has come to bring deliverance to those who need it most. It's joy for all and it's liberty and justice for all, especially for those who need it most. It's both/and.

Then there are the two sides of the coin about how to fulfill Jesus's mission. One side of the coin is works of mercy, compassion, and assistance. The other side of the coin is working for changes in our system that will make life fairer and more secure for everyone. It's both/and.

Finally, there are two sides of the coin that Jim Wallis lifts up regarding the two basic biblical convictions that should guide us as disciples and as citizens. One side of this coin is that we are created in the image of God, that each of us is of equal worth and value—a principle that undergirds our affirmation of the individual. The other side of the coin is the conviction that we are created not for ourselves alone but for community with God and one another—a principle that affirms our life in community. We are individuals and we are all members of one body; we all belong to the commonwealth. It's both/and.

So that's it in a nutshell, you might even say in a chestnut shell. It's what we are to be about as disciples and as citizens, as a church and as a nation. So . . . let's just do it.

Credo: E Pluribus Unum

The Rev. Dr. Robert A. Chesnut, Ph.D.

The Gayton Kirk, Presbyterian Church (U.S.A.)

Henrico, Virginia

July 24, 2016

THE CARTOON SHOWS A couple seated together at the breakfast table. She's nicely coiffed, dressed up, obviously ready to go out somewhere. He's still in pajamas, unshaved, hair a mess. He says, "Give me just one good reason I have to show up at that church every Sunday."

She replies, "You're the minister!"

So . . . I've been retired for 14 years now. I'm not the minister here. I really don't have to show up any Sunday at all. So why do I . . . show up?

A retired minister friend of mine has recently written a poem that speaks to this very question. By J. Barrie Sheppard, "Why I Still Go" includes lines that acknowledge every church's "quirks and quibbles . . . foibles and squabbles," our recalcitrance concerning one issue or another, and our reluctance, like those very first disciples, to accept "what fairest Jesus brought to life." The poet confesses to weariness that we keep coming here again and again, still "no closer to the kingdom," ever "hungering across years of disappointment." Yet despite the "continuing disillusion and despair," my friend finds himself pulled back, week after week, by "the same sweet songs" and "familiar prayers" and, most of all, by his hunger for words that might drag us all back again "to trust, compassion, even resolution."[2]

---

2. *The Presbyterian Outlook*, 8/8/2016.

I find myself here virtually every Sunday for the same reasons and because, most of all, being here reminds me of my identity, my Christian identity—who I am and what I'm living for. I've been showing up every Sunday since I was a child—and sometimes as a reluctant adolescent—because being here re-instills the virtues, values, and visions to which I have been committed all my life. Being here keeps alive in me the call of Jesus.

This is what I want us to reflect about today—our Christian identity. But that's not all. I want us to think also about how our Christian identity relates to our American identity. You might consider this a late Fourth of July sermon.

My approach this morning is going to be personal to start with. We'll get to the biblical part later. Now up front I confess that I come at this with some of the same disappointment, disillusion, and despair revealed in my friend's poem. These days I often find myself feeling a good bit of sadness—even to the point of tears—about the present state of affairs in our nation and in our world.

You see, at my age I grieve that I may not have much time left to see things turn around. I grieve about a world awash in hatred and weapons and unspeakable violence. I grieve about the all-too-often bitter, hateful divisions among us. I grieve that sometimes it feels like we're almost intent upon tearing ourselves apart. As a Christian I do hope and pray that we can find faithful, constructive ways to address our troubles, but we'll get to that later.

Right now, if you'll indulge me, I want to share a bit about my own life story. I think it can help to illustrate and illuminate some of the challenges facing us all. My American family history is Celtic in origin, going back to William Chesnut, who arrived in Virginia from Ireland in the mid-1700s. He fought for the Revolution. Later Chesnuts fought for the Confederacy. On my other side, my maternal great-great-grandfather owned a Virginia plantation with 125 slaves. My father was born in Indian Territory, two years before it became the state of Oklahoma. For a brief time in his teens, when I'd like to think that he really didn't know any better, he was a member of the KKK. I grew up in Oklahoma in a totally segregated small town. Blacks were there, but confined to the other side of the tracks. Native Americans were nearby, but confined to a reservation.

Consider how far I've come. On my wife's side, our family includes a large contingent of over two dozen Syrians. These are our nephews and nieces, great-nephews and nieces, great-great-nephews and nieces. All of them are Muslims. Most of them have fled Syria now. But some of them, including Jan's sister Elaine and her husband Mohammed, both in their eighties, still live in Damascus.

In addition, our family's diversity includes our dear Mexican-born daughter-in-law and her two Mexican-American sons. Our own two grandchildren are one-quarter Mexican, one-quarter Swiss, one-half Anglo. And . . . one immediate family member is gay.

For the final 14 years of my ministry I pastored an inner-city congregation in Pittsburgh that was in a predominantly black neighborhood and included a large contingent of African-American members. Our congregation, besides being black and white, embraced rich and poor, urbanites and suburbanites, gays and straights, liberals and conservatives, homeless people housed in our church shelter, plus some university and seminary professors. Our church was indeed a motley crew, a rich mixture of all sorts and conditions of folk.

After retiring from that congregation in 2002 we moved to Santa Fe, New Mexico, where we were enriched by the region's tri-cultural heritage of Hispanics, Native Americans, and Anglos. Our Presbyterian church there was a mix of Hispanics and Anglos, with lots of the Sunday service in Spanish. Many northern New Mexico families, by the way, can trace their Spanish heritage in this land back to the conquistadors, four hundred years or more. Santa Fe was founded in 1610, a decade before the Pilgrims landed.

Since moving here two years ago, Jan and I have lived in a new townhouse community in Short Pump. Our neighborhood is predominantly one of Indian-American families with a smattering of other Asians, African-Americans, Middle Easterners, and just a few whites. Our two nearest neighbor families are Kuwaiti Muslims. The women are PhD students in pharmacy at VCU and the men are stay-at-home dads with young kids. They are the nicest neighbors you could ever want.

During our years in Pittsburgh and well into retirement I served on the boards of two nationwide Presbyterian organizations. One, the Covenant Network, has worked for full inclusion of LGBT folk in the church. The other, the Presbyterian Multicultural Church network, has offered practical help and encouragement to congregations in reaching out to new populations, in becoming more diverse and inclusive in their membership, in breaking down barriers and building relationships across lines of race and class and nationality, and in welcoming immigrants.

Why? Why have I given my time and energies to such causes? So now we get biblical. It is because I passionately believe that's clearly what Jesus did, leading the way for his followers. Because that's what the Apostle Paul and the New Testament church did. Because that's the vision—from Genesis to Revelation—that we read about in our scriptures this morning.

You know we're still in the post-Pentecost season in our Christian calendar. You know that Pentecost—which we call the birthday of the church—is all about the gift of the Holy Spirit. On Pentecost the Spirit gave the apostles the gift of speaking in tongues. This enabled them to share the gospel in a universal language that could be understood by all the many different nationalities that were gathered in Jerusalem on Pentecost. Furthermore, that same day Peter announced that the Holy Spirit was giving the gift of dreaming dreams and seeing visions to all God's people—young and old, male and female, servants and masters alike.

However, if you remember some of our scriptures and sermons of a few weeks back, you recall that Peter himself had to be carried more or less kicking and screaming into the realization that the vision given at Pentecost was even wider than he thought, that the gift of the Gospel and of the Holy Spirit was not just for Jews. Christ was for everyone, for all the world.

Paul struggled with Peter to get him to see this wider vision. Then, finally, Peter was granted his own transforming vision, revealing to him that God was indeed drawing the circle of divine redeeming love far wider than Peter had at first imagined. Peter had his own conversion. He saw that he had been wrong. Paul was right. It was no longer all about being Jewish. By faith and in the Spirit anyone and everyone, all races and nationalities, could now be children of Abraham, heirs of the covenant. Paul was right: In Christ there is no Greek or Jew, slave or free, male or female, but we are all one.

So the early church rather quickly came to the realization that Christian identity was to be based not on race but on faith. It was faith, not race, that made them one in Christ.

Now the same thing is undeniably true of our American identity. As Americans, what unites us is not race. As Americans, what makes us one is not our ethnicity or subculture. What makes us one as Americans is our shared principles, our values, our convictions, our ideals. This is what enables us, inspires us, empowers us to reach out to embrace and affirm one another across all boundaries and barriers that might divide us, to draw our circle wide, to be one people. As Americans. As Christians.

A second point at which our Christian identity and our American identity overlap is our Christian conviction and our American conviction that our diversity makes us richer. *E pluribus unum* is our national motto . . . one out of many. It means that we do not aim for uniformity. We celebrate diversity in our unity. I believe that our national motto, our national conviction of *e pluribus unum,* has been inspired by our Christian notion of the body of Christ. We have many parts to our one body, says Paul, different parts with different functions, but every part makes its own contribution to building up the body, making the body whole and functioning. We need each other with all our differences. We enrich one another with all our differences. *E pluribus unum.*

Our different cultures and traditions make us richer. So it's okay, it's good to celebrate the Celtic tradition as we do here at the Kirk, or our African tradition, or our Native American culture, or our Asian heritage. This is not the old idea that so many of us grew up with, not the "melting pot" idea. The "melting pot" meant that everyone was supposed to be assimilated to the one dominant, homogeneous culture. That's what made us do some horrible things in the past, taking Native American children from their families, forcing them into boarding schools where their culture was stripped away and they were whipped for speaking their native language. I knew some older Native Americans in New Mexico who endured that as children in an Oklahoma boarding school.

Our more enlightened, more humane, more Christian ideal today is not the "melting pot" but the "mixed salad" or the "Brunswick stew." We're all together in one pot or one bowl in which our differences are valued and honored and celebrated—at the same affirming that we are indeed one nation, one people united by our overriding principles and values and convictions. It is okay to be a hyphenated American, a Native American or African-American or Indian-American or maybe even a Celtic-American. It's not either/or. We can be both/and. *E pluribus unum.*

These convictions are challenged today. We live in dangerous, frightening times at home and abroad. I know it can be tempting to give in to fear and despair and maybe even, God forbid, desperate measures. In some neighborhoods some people fear the police. And the police fear some people in some neighborhoods. In Pittsburgh we rebuilt a declining church in just such a neighborhood.

Some people fear and suspect those of a different race or religion. In stressful, fearful times it can be especially tempting to paint all people in another group with a broad brush—all Muslims, all blacks, all whites, all police. And sometimes our media and our politicians are tempted to exploit those fears and prejudices.

In the name of our basic identity, our basic values and beliefs—as Americans, as Christians—we simply must not succumb to such thinking. That's what happened in Nazi Germany and in Rwanda and in the former Yugoslavia. Sadly, shamefully, that's what happened in our own country at the start of World War II when we forced Japanese-Americans into detention camps, depriving them of their rights and liberties, their property and their livelihoods, simply because of their race and national origin.

There were two saving graces in my upbringing, two factors in my childhood that gave me a head start on the issues we've talked about this morning. One was our family's Christian faith. We did show up at that church every Sunday—that little white frame Presbyterian church where we renewed our identity, our faith, and our values. The second grace was my mother who, by light of her Christian faith, transcended the prejudices of her time and place. She believed that all people were equal as children of God; all people were our neighbors, to be loved just as we love ourselves. Never, ever did I hear her speak a negative word about another race or religion or nationality.

And, yes, thank God, my father did come around over time. Towards the end of his postal career, when he was serving as postmaster during the civil rights era, he saw that the black part of our town finally got the home delivery service they had long been denied.

May God grant us all—in the midst of horrifying events in our nation and our world, in the face of hateful speech and vitriol—may God grant us to stand fast in our basic identity, our Christian identity and our American identity. God grant us wisdom, God grant us courage to reach out and build bridges, not walls, between people. May we foster faith, hope, and love . . . not fear and despair. May we listen and seek to understand and work together with all our neighbors, all God's children whom Jesus calls us to love as we love ourselves, for the common good, for peace and justice for all.

Bibliography

Adams-Riley, Wallace. *The Epistle*. Richmond, VA: St. Paul's Episcopal Church, Feb/Mar 2016.

Allison, Dale C., Jr. *The Historical Christ and the Theological Jesus*. Grand Rapids, MI: Eerdmans, 2009. Kindle edition.

———. *Night Comes: Death, Imagination, and the Last Things*. Grand Rapids, MI: Eerdmans, 2016. Kindle edition.

Aslan, Reza. *Zealot: The Life and Times of Jesus of Nazareth*. New York: Random House, 2013.

Athanasius. *On the Incarnation of the Word*. New York: Macmillan, 1947.

Baillie, D.M. *God Was In Christ: An Essay on Incarnation and Atonement*. New York: Scribner, 1948.

Bell, Rob. *Love Wins*. New York: HarperCollins, 2011.

Bellah, Robert. "Civil Religion in America." *Daedalus*, 96 (1967): 1–19.

Billings, J. Todd. *Calvin, Participation, and the Gift*. New York: Oxford University Press, 2008.

Borg, Marcus J. *Convictions: How I Learned What Matters Most*. New York: HarperCollins, 2014.

Borg, Marcus J., and N. T. Wright. *The Meaning of Jesus: Two Visions*. New York: HarperCollins, 1999.

Boyarin, Daniel. *The Jewish Gospels: The Story of the Jewish Christ*. New York: New Press, 2012.

Carroll, James. *Christ Actually: The Son of God for the Secular Age*. New York: Viking/Penguin, 2014. Kindle edition.

Catechism of the Catholic Church. 2nd ed. Vatican City: Libreria Editrice Vaticana; Washington, D.C., U.S. Catholic Conference, 2000.

Chesnut, R. Andrew and Robert A. "Pope of Paradox." http://www.huffingtonpost.com/r-andrew-chesnut/pope-of-paradox_b_4295693.html

Chesnut, Robert A. "Modernization, Nationalism and Religious Commitment: An Exploratory Approach to the Study of Secularization." PhD diss., Harvard University, 1974.

———. *Transforming the Mainline Church: Lessons in Change from Pittsburgh's Cathedral of Hope*. Louisville: Geneva, 2000.

Cragg, Gerald R., ed. *The Works of John Wesley*, Vol. 11: *The Appeals to Men of Reason and Religion and Certain Related Open Letters*. Nashville: Abingdon, 1987.

Douglas, Deborah. Review of *The Rebirthing of God* by John Philip Newell. *Christian Century* 132 (24 Jun 2015): 41.

Erhman, Bart. *How Jesus Became God: Course Guidebook.* Chantilly, VA: The Great Courses, 2014.

Felten, David M., and Jeff Procter-Murphy. *Living the Questions: The Wisdom of Progressive Christianity.* New York: HarperCollins, 2012. PDF e-book.

Flood, Derek. *Healing the Gospel: A Radical Vision for Grace, Justice, and the Cross.* Eugene, OR: Cascade, 2012.

Friedman, Thomas L. "Dump G.O.P. for a Grand New Party." *New York Times,* June 8, 2016.

Glory to God. Louisville, KY: Westminster John Knox, 2013.

Gorman, Michael J. *Becoming the Gospel: Paul, Participation, and Mission.* Grand Rapids, MI: Eerdmans, 2015.

Hanson, J.W. *Universalism: The Prevailing Doctrine of the Christian Church During Its First Five Hundred Years.* Boston: Universalist Publishing House, 1899.

Hopper, Nate. "8 Questions." Interview with Bruce Feiler. *Time,* April 3, 2017, 64.

Irenaeus, *Against the Heresies.* Book III. Translated by Dominic J. Unger. Mahwah, NJ: Newman, 2012.

Jung, Carl. *Memories, Dreams, Reflections.* Translated by Richard and Clara Winston. New York: Pantheon, 1963.

John Paul II. "Orientale Lumen." Apostolic Letter of May 2, 1995. http://w2.vatican.va/content/john-paul-ii/en/apost_letters/1995/documents/hf_jp-ii_apl_19950502_orientale-lumen.html

Kristof, Nicholas. "Am I a Christian, Pastor Timothy Keller?" *New York Times,* December 23, 2016. Online edition.

Küng, Hans. *On Being a Christian.* Translated by Edward Quinn. Garden City, NY: Doubleday, 1976.

Lewis, C. S. *Letters to Malcolm: Chiefly on Prayer.* New York: Harcourt, Brace & World, 1964.

MacDonald, Gregory. *The Evangelical Universalist.* Second edition. Eugene, OR: Cascade, 2012.

Meyers, Robin. *The Underground Church: Reclaiming the Subversive Way of Jesus.* San Francisco: Jossey-Bass, 2012.

Nadler, Allan. "What Jesus Wasn't: Zealot." *Jewish Review of Books,* August 11, 2013. Online edition https://jewishreviewofbooks.com/articles/449/reza-aslan-what-jesus-wasnt/.

Nelson, Susan L. *Healing the Broken Heart: Sin, Alienation, and the Gift of Grace.* St. Louis: Chalice, 1997.

Newell, John Phillip. *Listening for the Heartbeat of God: A Celtic Spirituality.* Mahwah, NJ: Paulist Press, 1997.

———. *A New Harmony: The Spirit, the Earth and the Human Soul.* San Francisco: Jossey-Bass, 2011.

Nouwen, Henri. *Thomas Merton: Contemplative Critic.* San Francisco: Harper and Row, 1981.

———. *The Wounded Healer.* New York: Random House, 1979.

Ortberg, John. "Category Confusion: Is the Question for Christians 'Out or In?' or 'Farther or Closer?'" *Christianity Today* (June 2010) online edition. http://www.christianitytoday.com/pastors/2010/june-online-only/categoryconfusion.html

Pagett, Doug. "10 Things I Wish Everyone Knew about Progressive Evangelicals." https://www.onfaith.co/onfaith/2015/02/19/10-things-i-wish-everyone-knew-about-progressive-evangelicals/36195.

Pelikan, Jaroslav. *Jesus Through the Centuries: His Place in the History of Culture.* New Haven: Yale University Press, 1999.

Rohr, Richard. *Dancing Standing Still: Healing the World from a Place of Prayer.* Mahwah, NJ: Paulist, 2014.

————. *Immortal Diamond: The Search for Our True Self.* San Francisco: Jossey-Bass, 2013.

Rutledge, Fleming. *The Crucifixion: Understanding the Death of Jesus Christ.* Grand Rapids, MI: Eerdmans, 2015.

Schweitzer, Albert. *The Quest of the Historical Jesus.* London: A. and C. Black, 1911.

Tournier, Paul. *A Place for You: Psychology and Religion.* New York: Harper and Row, 1968.

Talbott, Thomas. *The Inescapable Love of God.* Second edition. Eugene, OR: Cascade, 2014.

Wallis, Jim. *On God's Side: What Religion Forgets and Politics Hasn't Learned about Serving the Common Good.* Grand Rapids, MI: Brazos, 2013. Kindle edition.

Walls, Jerry L. *Purgatory: The Logic of Total Transformation.* New York: Oxford University Press, 2012.

Warren, Mervyn A. *King Came Preaching: The Pulpit Power of Dr. Martin Luther King Jr.* Downers Grove, IL: InterVarsity, 2001.